INVADERS

of the Great Lakes

Produced in cooperation with Wildlife Forever
by Karen R. Hollingsworth

Adventure Publications, Inc.
Cambridge, Minnesota

DEDICATION

To our waters and those who work tirelessly to protect them.

– Karen Hollingsworth

Acknowledgments

Technical Editors: Philip B. Moy, Ph.D., Assistant Director for Research and Outreach, Fisheries and Invasive Species Specialist, Wisconsin Sea Grant Institute and a committee from the Great Lakes Sea Grant Network

Project Coordinator: Pat Conzemius, Conservation Director, Wildlife Forever

Cover and book design by Jonathan Norberg

Photo credits on page 151

The second edition printing of this field guide was made possible by Great Lakes Restoration Initiative grant funds from USEPA and USFWS.

10 9 8 7 6 5 4 3 2

of the Great Lakes

ABOUT WILDLIFE FOREVER

Wildlife Forever is America's leading all-species nonprofit conservation organization. Working with private conservation groups, state game and fish departments and federal agencies, Wildlife Forever has been involved in more than 1,000 projects, covering every state in the nation.

Wildlife Forever's conservation projects fall into four categories: habitat, fish and wildlife management, research, and conservation education. Award-winning programs include the Threat Campaign™, which provides anglers, hunters and all recreational users with the information they need to stop the spread of invasive species, and THE ART OF CONSERVATION® State-Fish Art™ Program, a K-12 nationwide competition teaching children aquatic education through the arts.

America is truly blessed. It is a land rich in natural resources. Much of our identity and culture can be attributed to our natural world. We believe conservation education is the key that will ultimately determine the very future of our country's fish and wildlife heritage.

Conserving America's fisheries, by preventing the introduction and spread of invasive species, is more critical than ever before. Anglers and recreationists need to know the risks and what to do when they encounter invasive species in the wild. These silent invaders are serious threats, and they are damaging fishing, destroying habitat, devastating the aquatic food chain, impeding navigation, and costing the American public millions of dollars annually. This guide describes the top invasive threats to the Great Lakes and highlights the steps everyone can take to help prevent their spread.

Thank you for doing your part to ensure the healthy future of our lakes and streams . . .

Douglas H. Grann
President & CEO

4

To learn more, contact us at (763) 253-0222, 2700 Freeway Blvd., Suite 1000, Brooklyn Center, MN 55430 or check out our website at www.WildlifeForever.org.

ABOUT SEA GRANT

Sea Grant—a unique partnership of public and private sectors that combines research, education and technology transfer for public service—is a national network of universities meeting the changing environmental and economic needs of Americans in coastal ocean and Great Lakes regions.

Sea Grant has an outstanding record of achievement in transferring the results of university research to a wide range of audiences and giving special assistance to coastal communities, businesses and individual citizens.

Congressional committees have repeatedly cited Sea Grant as one of the most efficient and cost-effective programs funded by the U.S. Government. A 1981 analysis, for example, estimated that the annual benefits to the national economy from Sea Grant-sponsored research and outreach surpassed the federal government's total investment in the program over the preceding 12 years, and the program's benefits continue to grow exponentially.

Through its network of Advisory Service (Extension) agents and its use of modern communications and education techniques, the Great Lakes Sea Grant Network plays a central role in supplying the region and the nation with usable solutions to pressing problems and providing the basic information needed to better manage Great Lakes resources for present and future generations of Americans.

For more information, visit www.seagrant.noaa.gov.

TABLE OF CONTENTS

FOREWORD

Aquatic invasive species are hitchhikers, and their spread is not inevitable. Those of us who do business or spend time on or around the water can unintentionally help aquatic invasive species spread. They can be visible as plant fragments or adult organisms clinging to a boat or trailer, or they can be microscopic and float in bilge water, a livewell or a bait bucket. By learning about how these organisms live, grow and reproduce—and how they spread—boaters and anglers can learn how to stop aquatic hitchhikers!

Reducing their spread is vitally important. Prevention saves money and jobs, and protects lakes and rivers and the outdoor heritage that we all enjoy. It helps give researchers time to discover and develop ways to manage, control or possibly eradicate these unwanted visitors. We all have a responsibility to care for and manage our nation's waters and to help educate others about the importance of preventing the spread of aquatic invasive species.

This guide is the product of a partnership among the programs of the Great Lakes Sea Grant Network, Wildlife Forever, the U.S. Forest Service, the U.S. Fish and Wildlife Service and the National Professional Anglers Association. Working together, we strive to help the boating and angling public learn about the threat aquatic invasive species pose to our environment and economy, and what we can do to prevent their spread.

Join me and our partners in the fight to protect our treasured fishing and boating waters so we can ensure they are here for this generation and those that follow.

Philip B. Moy, Ph.D.
Assistant Director for Research and Outreach
Fisheries and Invasive Species Specialist
University of Wisconsin Sea Grant Institute

ENDORSEMENT

For the past 18 years I have been truly blessed to make my living as a professional angler. I get to travel the country and enjoy the great fishing we have literally coast to coast. There is nothing better. At this time, we are very fortunate. I have never seen fishing as good as it is today, nationwide.

From time to time, things come along that threaten the opportunities we have to enjoy this incredible fishing. In the past few decades, aquatic invasive species have become a major concern. These undesirable plants and animals are brought to our waters unintentionally and threaten to destroy the pastime we all love so dearly.

The Great Lakes were the first areas devastated by them, but now many inland waterways are threatened. From zebra mussels and Eurasian watermilfoil to many fish species, there seems to be no end. No one knows what the next threat will be or where it will come from.

There is hope, however. The spread of these species can be controlled, and it starts with us—the anglers—because we care. By learning to recognize aquatic invasive species, inspecting our boats and trailers, and draining our livewells and bilges, we can help prevent the spread of these threats.

As a member of the National Professional Anglers Association, I am proud to join forces with the Great Lakes Sea Grant Network, Wildlife Forever, the U.S. Forest Service and the U.S. Fish and Wildlife Service in the creation of this guide. Carry it with you and keep a lookout for these species, which threaten our favorite pastime. Please report invasives when you see them and pass the word on stopping their spread.

I personally thank you and hope to see you on the water.

Johnnie Candle
Professional Angler
2010 World Walleye Champion

AQUATIC INVASIVE SPECIES: THREATS TO THE GREAT LAKES

The Great Lakes and our inland lakes, rivers and streams are being invaded. Since the 1800s, more than 180 non-native aquatic organisms of all types—including plants, fish, invertebrates and pathogens—have become established in the Great Lakes region. Some, such as coho salmon, were purposely stocked, while others were inadvertently introduced after hitching rides in freshwater ballast of ocean-going ships, anglers' bait-buckets or on recreational watercraft.

When a non-native species is introduced to a new ecosystem and causes, or is likely to cause, economic or environmental harm or harm to human health, it's considered invasive. Because non-native species are adept at surviving in different ecosystems, some have advantages for outcompeting our native species for food and habitat. Without predators, diseases and competitors to keep these species in check, they rapidly grow, reproduce and spread. This can lead to significant damage to the entire ecosystem. When such species reproduce unchecked, this can lead to significant changes to the native food web, which is in a fragile balance. When a new species is introduced, it can disrupt that balance, causing a cascade of problems for all the interconnected species.

Unfortunately, over the past two centuries, a whole host of invasive species has ravaged the Great Lakes, profoundly harming the region's economy, recreational opportunities and biodiversity. Native fish species that were once economically important, such as the lake trout, have been decimated, costing commercial fishermen millions and denying recreational anglers a prized target. Once-tidy boats and harbors are now littered with thousands upon thousands of zebra mussels, which are almost impossible to control. Water-intake pipes at power plants and factories are choked with quagga mussels. Pristine lakes are now matted with invasive species, such as Eurasian watermilfoil or elodea, reducing property values and making fishing and enjoying time on the water difficult, if not impossible.

Hitching a Ride: How They Got Here
Many of the aquatic invasive species in the region "hitch-hiked" here. Completion of the St. Lawrence Seaway in the 1950s connected the Great Lakes to the Atlantic Ocean, enabling immature fish and invertebrates to "stow away" in

ballast tanks of ocean-going ships or attach to hull surfaces. A number of species made their way here in this fashion. Examples include the round goby (page 101), tubenose goby (page 103), spiny waterflea (page 67), fishhook waterflea (page 65), bloody red shrimp (page 55) and a host of other invertebrates and plants. In addition, the completion of shipping canals allowed saltwater and salt-tolerant species, such as alewife (page 91), to enter the Great Lakes. For example, the sea lamprey (page 107), which is native to the Atlantic Coast, entered the upper Great Lakes through the Welland Canal, devastating the fisheries in all of the Great Lakes.

Thankfully, we've made progress in preventing new species from entering the region. In 1993, the U.S. Coast Guard began requiring all ocean-going ships bound for the Great Lakes carrying ballast water to perform an open-ocean ballast exchange. They do this because salty ocean water kills freshwater organisms taken on in European harbors. Later, in 2008, ships carrying cargo were likewise required to do a "swish and spit" with ocean water. These regulations and policies have greatly reduced the threat, and no new Great Lake invasive species attributable to ballast discharge have been discovered since 2006.

A Danger to Inland Waters
While we've made progress in preventing additional species from entering the region, the species that are already here pose a serious threat to our inland lakes, rivers and streams. Just as they invaded the Great Lakes, they could easily invade thousands of inland water bodies across the region.

Instead of hitching a ride in ballast water or swimming up a man-made waterway, invasive species, such as Eurasian watermilfoil, could easily be introduced inadvertently by anglers, boaters and any people enjoying time on the water. Unless proper inspection and washing steps are taken (see page 20), it's easy to accidentally transport an invasive species. They can hitch a ride on (or in) trailers, boats, motors, livewells or other angling or boating equipment that comes into contact with invasive-infested water. Unfortunately, this isn't simply a threat. Many inland bodies of water have already been infested with aquatic invasives, and it's up to us to prevent them from spreading even more.

Natural Treasures to Protect
When we protect our aquatic environments, we're actually putting our own interests first. After all, the Great Lakes and our inland lakes have contributed a great deal to our region. The region became a major population center and the industrial core of the United States and Canada in large part because of the region's vast forests and its agricultural and mineral resources.

Today, the Great Lakes region is as important as ever, but aquatic invasive species pose a serious threat to the lakes and to our inland waterways. Unfortunately, when it comes to invaders (such as zebra mussels and Asian carp), it's often an all-or-nothing game. Once the invaders are established, they are likely here to stay. That's why it's so important to spread the word about stopping aquatic invasive species.

Here are just a few reasons to join the fight:

Economic Impact

The Great Lakes have a profound economic impact on the region. A 2011 analysis by the University of Michigan Sea Grant Program concluded that the Great Lakes generate $62 billion in wages each year and that more than 1.5 million jobs are directly connected to the waterways. That economic impact is hard to miss; commercial ports, fishing ports and recreational harbors are common sights. Not surprisingly, the lakes are also a major water source in the region and provide water for about 30 million people.

Recreational and Commercial Fishing on the Great Lakes

Several Great Lakes boast thriving recreational fisheries that are based on salmon, which were introduced to the lakes in the 1960s to control alewives. Today, the fisheries of the Great Lakes have an estimated value of $7 billion. Salmon continue to be stocked, but they have also begun to spawn on their own in rivers and streams that flow into the Great Lakes.

The Great Lakes are also home to a commercial fishery that is mainly supported by whitefish, yellow perch and lake herring. It harvested more than $18 million worth of fish in 2009, according to a report from the U.S. Geological Survey's Great Lakes Science Center.

Fishing on Inland Lakes, Regional Tourism, and Biodiversity

The fight against aquatic invasives isn't just about the Great Lakes, however. The Great Lakes are a case study in aquatic invasive species introduction and impact, and the Great Lakes are often a source of invasive species that can spread to inland lakes. Our treasured inland lakes, rivers and streams are very much at risk, and when invasives are introduced, they can have a profound impact. Iconic fish and waterfowl species can be adversely affected, the chemistry of the water can be irreparably changed, and even enjoying time on the water can be difficult due to mats of vegetation. Infested waters can harm tourism, fishing, property values and the economy of communities that depend upon those water resources.

THREE PRIMARY AQUATIC THREATS: INVERTEBRATES, PLANTS AND FISH

Three types of aquatic invasive species pose the greatest threat to the Great Lakes and our inland waterways: Invertebrates, Plants and Fish. As each type of invasive can be introduced in a different way, each type poses a different threat. For instance, invasive fish species can be introduced when they are accidentally used for bait, while invasive invertebrates, such as spiny waterfleas, can be moved when improperly cleaned gear is used in uninfested waters. It's therefore important to know what to look for, where to look and what to do to help stop the spread of aquatic invasive species.

Aquatic Invertebrates

Invertebrates are some of the most abundant creatures on earth—about 97 percent of all known living animal species—yet they are often inconspicuous and few people are aware of their presence, much less their importance.

Wildly diverse creatures, the only thing they all have in common is what they lack—a backbone. They are everywhere, and they outnumber us. In fact, the combined body mass of just the insects and spiders in the United States, it would be more than twice that of humans.

Aquatic invertebrates are threatened, yet they play critical roles in healthy ecosystems. In the United States an estimated 50 percent or more of crayfish, freshwater mussel and stonefly species are imperiled, near extinction or already extinct.

There is a critical need to protect native aquatic invertebrates from the effects of habitat destruction and displacement by invasive species. Impacts on such important food resources have serious repercussions throughout the aquatic food web.

Aquatic Plants

Thousands of species of aquatic plants are native to the United States. As an essential part of a healthy ecosystem, their presence in a body of water is one of the best indicators that it will be a good fishery. These plants produce the oxygen vital for life, help reduce erosion and provide nutrients. Most aquatic life also depends upon plants for food. They also provide fish with cover, nursery areas and protection.

When aquatic plants are introduced into a new environment, they can become invasive. Invasive aquatic plants often grow very quickly, and a population can go from just a few plants, or even fragments, to potentially cover hundreds of acres in a short time. This chokes out native plants, eliminates useful habitat for fish and other wildlife, disrupts recreational activities, reduces tourism and lowers property values.

Once an invasive is established, attempts to eradicate it often fail and management is very expensive. That is why preventing their spread is critically important.

Fish
More than 32,000 species of fish live in the world's water and roughly 2,000 species live in North America alone.

Unfortunately in the United States, approximately 37 percent of freshwater fish species are threatened or even extinct. The worst invasive species have caused substantial damage to Great Lakes fisheries and ecosystem health by taking over the habitat and food that native fish species need to survive.

In addition, invasive species, such as zebra mussels (page 53) and quagga mussels (page 51), are in danger of unraveling the food web because they consume huge amounts of phytoplankton, the base of the food web. This essentially starves native fish and other aquatic wildlife. So while the Great Lakes seem cleaner and clearer than ever before, cleaner is good, but clearer isn't. The water looks clear because it is becoming less productive.

EDUCATION IS THE KEY

The most important weapon in the fight against aquatic invasive species is education—informing the public how to prevent them from spreading. Studies show that anglers, boaters and other people who enjoy time on the water will take the time to clean, drain and dry their boats, trailers, tackle and gear if they know the threats, what to look for and what to do. It is equally important to show anglers, boaters and all who spend time on the water that proactive prevention is the most effective method of stopping the spread of aquatic invasives.

Tournament Anglers Need to Be Aware

Tournament anglers need to be especially careful about inadvertent transport of aquatic invasives. Professional tournament anglers may visit dozens of waters in multiple states each year as they pre-fish, compete, then quickly travel long distances to the next tournament site. While most competitive anglers strive for clean gear, the sheer number of anglers and lakes visited raises concern about the potential for accidental spread to uninfested waters.

Thankfully, tournament anglers are willing to be part of the solution by taking action at accesses and teaching fellow anglers about the risks posed by aquatic invasive species. Professional anglers are familiar with our native aquatic plants and animals, and they often have a keen eye for that weed or fish that looks a bit out of the ordinary.

Keep a Lookout

But it's not just anglers who need to take care. Invasive species can enter our aquatic ecosystems in a variety of other ways. Any human activity that potentially moves water, soil, mud, sand, weeds or animals could possibly transport aquatic invasive species. Potential pathways include aquarium releases, bait harvesting, boating, hunting, scuba diving, seaplanes and personal watercraft. We all have a responsibility to protect our natural waters from the threat of aquatic invasive species.

HOW YOU CAN HELP

1. **CLEAN • DRAIN • DRY!** Don't let invasives hitchhike on your watercraft or equipment.

2. Know state and federal regulations (see page 22)

3. Identify—learn what aquatic invasives look like by using this guide

4. Keep up to date on where invasives are by referencing the QR codes (page 31) and websites (page 124) in this book

5. Report any suspected new sightings

1. CLEAN • DRAIN • DRY

BE A PART OF THE SOLUTION!
You can help stop the invasion.

STOP AQUATIC HITCHHIKERS!™

Boaters, anglers and other outdoor recreationists can help prevent the spread of aquatic invasive species by taking three simple actions— **CLEAN • DRAIN • DRY**—every time they are at the water access. If drying is not possible before reuse, rinsing or washing watercraft and equipment is the right thing to do. Rinsing removes small organisms that may not be visible. Washing with hot water kills small organisms that may not be visible. By taking these actions whether the water is infested or not, you are part of the solution and helping ensure that our lakes and rivers will be healthy for future generations.

BEFORE launching . . . BEFORE leaving:

CLEAN your watercraft, trailer, motor, equipment, clothing, boots, buckets. Remove all visible mud, aquatic plants and animals before leaving any water access.

DRAIN water from your boat, bilge, motor, jet drives and livewell by removing the drain plug and opening all water-draining devices away from the boat ramp. In many states and provinces, this is required when leaving water accesses. Remove water from any bait buckets, diving gear, boots/waders, floats and any other gear.

DRY everything at least five days before going to other waters or spray/rinse recreational equipment with high pressure and/or hot water.

All three of these steps are equally important, as it's what you might not see that counts! The larvae of zebra mussels (veligers) and many other species are often microscopic or easy to overlook. These tiny organisms can live for days in water left in boat hulls, livewells and bait buckets. If transported to new waters, they can grow into adults, reproduce, and spread, threatening our favorite fishing spots.

2. Know the Regulations

Because aquatic invasive species are such a prominent threat, laws specifically pertaining to invasive species exist at the state, federal, provincial and sometimes local levels prohibiting possession, transport and spread. So it's about doing the right thing to help protect our lakes and rivers while being in compliance with the laws. Not taking appropriate action can result in citations and fines. Transporting invasives, even inadvertently, is often against the law.

For details and a list of prohibited aquatic invasive species in your area, check with your state natural resource department and local authorities. Also visit the following websites for more information. Also be mindful of Canadian regulations when fishing on or near the border, or when in Canada.

State:
Laws and regulations vary state-by-state. For specific information about your state, we have provided a list of Sea Grant and state websites on page 124.

Federal:
National Invasive Species Information Center
www.invasivespeciesinfo.gov/laws/federal.shtml

U.S. Fish and Wildlife Service
www.fws.gov/invasives/laws.html

Provincial:

If you are on or near Canadian waters, be sure to check these websites:

Ontario Ministry of Natural Resources
www.mnr.gov.on.ca/en

Ontario Federation of Anglers and Hunters
www.ofah.org

3. Identifying Invasives

This guide describes 39 aquatic invaders of concern in the Great Lakes region. These invaders could spread by hitching a ride on a boat motor, trailer or hull, when inadvertently transported in water, in contaminated bait or on angling equipment. All of these species pose threats to your favorite lakes and rivers. Each species page describes where each invader lives, grows, reproduces and spreads. In turn, this knowledge will help you understand how important it is to follow the three steps to Stop Aquatic Hitchhikers on page 20.

4. Keep Up to Date with QR (Quick Response) Codes

Quick and easy access to basic information about aquatic invasive species is just a click away. For smartphones, scan the QR code (the funny-looking square) on the lower left corner of each species page. For barcode applications, open the application and slowly pass the phone over the barcode, which will link to a webpage with up-to-date information about the aquatic invasive species.

5. Reporting . . . What Should You Do?

If you suspect a new sighting, report it. Reporting invasive species allows authorities to step up enforcement, outreach and communication efforts to help contain the spread and, if necessary, it can help scientists develop a plan to contain or control invaders. It also helps other boaters, anglers and folks who enjoy time on the water to stay up-to-date.

To help you report a sighting, we've included a "How You Can Help" section for each of the invaders in this book. This section provides species-specific steps for you to follow when reporting a find, as well as instructions about how to preserve a specimen. We have also included a "Template for Noting Sighting Details" on page 128 with fill-in-the-blank forms for you to easily jot down information to report to your local or state's natural resource agency. You will find a contact list for each state's natural resource agency on page 124.

For your convenience, you can also report a sighting online from anywhere in the United States at this link:

Great Lakes Aquatic Nonindigenous Species Information System (GLANSIS):
https://nas.er.usgs.gov/SightingReport.aspx

To find out more about aquatic invasive species and how you can help, visit the GLANSIS definitive database of non-native invaders. You can visit their website here:
www.glerl.noaa.gov/res/Programs/glansis/glansis.html

To discover what Wildlife Forever's Stop Aquatic Hitchhikers!-Threat Campaign™ has done to educate people and help prevent the spread of aquatic invasive species, visit: www.WildlifeForever.org.

WHAT'S NEXT? ARE MORE INVADERS ON THE WAY?

Our aggressive prevention and control efforts have been effective in keeping some aquatic invasive species at bay. What we do know is that if we do nothing, aquatic invasive species will spread and have a devastating impact. If we do all that we can, we will be able to continue to prevent and slow their spread. Being vigilant as good stewards will prevent existing aquatic invasive species from spreading to nearby lakes and rivers, and will prevent them from entering our region. Every water body that is protected helps our society, environment and economy.

Using information about life cycles of foreign species, living requirements, potential for range expansion, and how closely their home habitat resembles our native waterways, scientists predict that about two dozen additional non-native fish could arrive and thrive in our lakes, rivers and streams. At least nine of these could spread quickly, and five would likely harm native species. The wild card here is their ability to hitch a ride to North America; they could arrive via ship ballast, release by aquarists, escape from water gardens, or release of unwanted bait. If you find or catch something you don't recognize, report it.

Here Are the "Dangerous 5" Potential Invaders

In addition to Asian carp, we don't know for sure whether these "Dangerous 5" will make it into the Great Lakes region or not. Nevertheless, they have successfully invaded other countries and caused a great deal of damage in invaded territories, so we must continue to take every precaution to keep them out. These are the species to be on the lookout for; to that end, we're including a little information about each. If you think you've spotted one, report it!

Kilka (*Clupeonella cultriventris*): A potential ballast invader and a member of the herring family, it lives in rivers, lakes and the ocean. About 5½ inches long, it forms schools, eats zooplankton, and may compete with larval fish. Upon introduction, it would likely take over lakes and rivers, crowding out native fish.

Black-striped pipefish (*Syngnathus abaster*): Related to seahorses, they have slender bodies with bony rings. Males rear the young in pouches. They can live in both fresh and salt water and feed heavily on small benthic invertebrates and are capable of producing several broods of young over the year.

Black Sea silverside (*Atherina boyeri*): Also called bigscale sand smelt, it is found in slow-flowing or still water. It can survive in brackish water, as well as salt water and fresh water. It forms dense schools, feeding on crustaceans, worms, mollusks and fish larvae. It can grow to more than 7 inches long.

Monkey goby (*Neogobius fluviatalis*): Sold in the aquarium trade, it lives on sandy bottoms in near-shore areas of lakes and rivers. It also lives in brackish waters. Infestations can double each year, often becoming the most numerous fish in rivers. Growing only up to 8 inches long, it feeds on small clams, mussels and snails.

Caspian bighead goby (*Ponticola gorlap*): This species inhabits both fresh and brackish habitats in rivers, tributaries and inshore areas of lakes and coastal areas. It lives in a variety of habitats, including rocky, sandy-bottomed areas, reeds and aquatic vegetation. It eats invertebrates and small fish, including the young of other goby species. It can live 2–3 years and can reach 3–6 inches in length.

For images and information about these species, visit www.fishbase.org.

FISH DISEASES AND PARASITES AND HOW WE CAN HELP PREVENT THEIR SPREAD

Invasive fish, plants and invertebrates aren't the only organisms that can spread and invade a new environment. Like people, fish are vulnerable to a variety of diseases and parasites. Fish diseases are usually caused by organisms (pathogens), such as bacteria, viruses and fungi. Like aquatic invasive species, diseases and parasites can be transported from one body of water to another. This often happens via bait-bucket transfer. Putting bait in a body of water where a virus is present exposes the bait to that virus. Simply moving the fish to clean water does not remove the pathogen from the bait; on the contrary, that could transfer it to a new body of water. Aquatic plants can also carry diseases or pathogens. Likewise, invasive invertebrates, such as crayfish and snails, can carry diseases (such as crayfish plague) or be intermediate hosts for harmful parasites for native invertebrates. Anglers must be aware of the risks associated with moving fish, bait bucket water and invertebrates.

When fish are exposed to new pathogens, the disease often spreads quickly. Like human maladies, fish diseases are infectious: once a few fish get sick, the pathogens can spread rapidly from fish to fish, causing large die-offs. Examples of common fish diseases are the largemouth bass virus, bacterial kidney disease, *Heterosporis* and whirling disease. New diseases of concern in our waterways include viral hemorrhagic septicemia (VHS), spring viremia of carp, and koi herpes virus.

Diseases may affect fish in different ways, but many have similar symptoms that are easy to recognize. Here are a few common warning signs:

- Abnormal swimming in circles or upside down

- Gasping, rapid gill movement, bleeding, eroded or pale gills

- Skinny body, hollow belly

- Pale body colors

- External cysts, sores, blood stains, bloody or bulging eyes

- Fungus, often resembling white or yellow fuzz on body

Parasites are a problem, too. Generally, parasites don't kill the fish, but feed from them instead. When fish are stressed, parasites can further weaken the fish, making it more vulnerable to disease. Typical fish parasites include flukes, round worms, tapeworms and *Heterosporis*. Sometimes fish exhibit external signs that parasites are present, such as black flecks on the skin and fins or wormy threads inside the body, especially on internal organs.

To protect our waters from fish diseases and pathogens, be on the watch for fish that appear sick and report any suspicious sightings to your local fisheries manager. In some cases, humans can contract fish parasites by eating undercooked fish.

HOW TO USE THIS GUIDE

The species in this guide are divided into three categories: Invertebrates, Plants and Fish. For your convenience, we have also included an extensive Glossary (page 136); words that may be helpful to have defined are in **bold face** throughout the guide.

1. Learn to recognize these species, paying special attention to their appearance, their habits and their habitat.

2. If you find a suspected invader, first determine if it's an invertebrate, an aquatic plant, or a fish, then turn to that section.

3. Compare the suspected invader to the various species in that section.

4. If you're convinced that you've found a new sighting, refer to www.invasivespeciesinfo.gov to determine the current range of the suspect.

   If you have a smartphone and the Quick Response (QR) app, scan the QR code on that page. Once scanned, your phone will access a website that contains up-to-date information about the invasive species and documented infestations.

   The QR codes in the fish and invertebrate sections link to the United States Geological Survey's Nonindigenous Aquatic Species Database.

   The QR codes in the plants section link to the National Oceanic and Atmospheric Administration's Great Lakes Environmental Research Lab.

5. If the suspect has not been reported in your area, please follow the reporting procedures mentioned in the account of that species.

Remember to be good stewards—**CLEAN • DRAIN • DRY**—and keep this guide handy.

To Use the Quick Response Codes
1. Scan the code in the book with your smart phone . . .

2. which will take you to one of the following websites:

   the USGS Nonindigenous Aquatic Species (NAS) Database
   or
   NOAA's Great Lakes Environmental Research Lab (GLERL)

3. where you will find additional information, including a map of the species' native and invasive ranges.

Fishing line with clump of spiny waterfleas

Individual spiny waterflea enlarged 1,000 times

IMPACT ON YOU!

The potential or documented impact the invader has on anglers, boaters and other people who enjoy time on the water.

QR CODES: (QR IS SHORT FOR "QUICK RESPONSE")

Quick and easy access to basic information about aquatic invasive species is just a click away. For smartphones, scan the QR code (the funny-looking square) on the lower left corner of each species page.

For barcode applications, open the application and slowly pass the phone over the barcode, which will link to a webpage with up-to-date information about the aquatic invasive species.

Common name
Scientific name

OTHER COMMON NAMES: other names used to refer to the species

DESCRIPTION: the characteristics that can be used to identify the species; characteristics are usually visible without magnification

COMPARE: species that are similar in appearance to, or might be mistaken for, the species; includes information on how to differentiate them

HABITAT: local environment in which the species lives; includes food, water, cover (shelter) and space

ORIGIN: the continent or region of the world where the species is native and how it was introduced to the Great Lakes

SPREAD BY: describes how the invader can be spread by people from one location to another by human-related activity (e.g., transport via recreational boating, bait-bucket transfers, release of aquarium pets into waterways, etc.)

HOW YOU CAN HELP:

Describes what you can do to help prevent the spread of aquatic invasive species. Species-specific guidelines are provided to help you prevent their spread, as well as steps to report and document new sightings.

A fun fact or a highlight about the invasive species.

AQUATIC INVERTEBRATES

Aquatic invertebrates can be found in nearly any habitat, from small temporary pools to large lakes and small springs to large rivers. They are the small animals, such as insects, crustaceans, mollusks and worms, that live in the lower portion of the water column. Environmental bellwethers, they have been studied for years to assess the health of our streams, lakes, rivers and wetlands.

In fact, freshwater ecosystems support an amazing diversity of invertebrate life. There may be hundreds of individual animals and many different species living in a single square meter! They break down materials in the water, such as leaves and algae, and consume bacteria, fungus and dead animals, making energy and nutrients available to other invertebrates and fish.

Invertebrate Anatomy

For protection, invertebrates generally have a shell or a hard exoskeleton, but not always! Mussels and clams are mollusks, and their bodies have a pair of hard shells. Each shell is called a **valve**, and because

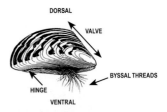

DORSAL

VALVE

BYSSAL THREADS

HINGE

VENTRAL

they have two valves, they are referred to as bivalves. An elastic part of the shell, called the **hinge**, connects the two halves and allows it to open and close. **Byssal threads** are strong, silky fibers that mussels and other bivalves secrete from a gland in their foot and use to attach themselves to rocks, pilings and other surfaces. They also use them to attach to each other, forming large colonies.

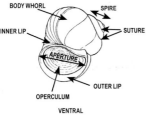

Like clams and mussels, snails are also a soft-bodied mollusk and are protected by a hard shell made up of coils. Each complete coil in the shell is called a **whorl**. The line that forms along any two overlapping whorls is a **suture** and the top of the shell is called the spire. The snail's body comes out through the **aperture**, the hole at the base of the shell, which is edged by **lips**. Some snails have an **operculum**, which is like a "trapdoor" that can close over the aperture after the snail has drawn itself inside.

The crayfish is a **crustacean** and has an exoskeleton (carapace) for protection and support. The abdomen is the segmented tail area and the triangular telson is the center of the tail fan. A crayfish moves using four pairs of long, jointed walking legs that are also used to probe for food. It swims forward using five pairs of short swimmerets

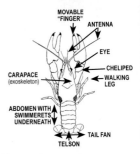

MOVABLE "FINGER"
ANTENNA
EYE
CHELIPED
CARAPACE (exoskeleton)
WALKING LEG
ABDOMEN WITH SWIMMERETS UNDERNEATH
TAIL FAN
TELSON

underneath the abdomen and backward by pushing water forward with its tail fan. The head has a pair of movable "eye stalks" and two pairs of antennae. When it moves, the crayfish holds out a pair of claw-bearing chelipeds. These are used for seizing food, and are useful when attacking prey or defending themselves.

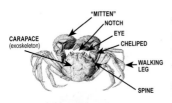

"MITTEN"
NOTCH
EYE
CHELIPED
CARAPACE (exoskeleton)
WALKING LEG
SPINE

The Chinese mitten crab is the only crab in this guide. When mitten crabs are large, you'll notice their "hairy" claws. These thick patches of setae, or bristles, give them their "mitten" name. Mitten crabs have a notch between the eyes and four spines on each side of the carapace. Mitten crabs walk on four pairs of long legs that are more than twice the carapace's width.

IMPACT ON YOU!

Large colonies of Asiatic clams can **biofoul** industrial and residential water-intake pipes. The high cost of removal (more than $1 billion annually) is passed on to consumers.

- Intensive **filter-feeders** that consume the microscopic plants and animals that many juvenile fish require in order to survive
- May dominate and displace the native bottom-dwelling species
- **Algal blooms** above the mussel bed

For more information go to www.usgs.gov or scan this code with your smart phone. See page 31 for details.

Asiatic clam
Corbicula fluminea

OTHER COMMON NAMES: Asian clam, prosperity clam

DESCRIPTION: 1–2 inches; yellowish to blackish-brown thick, triangular shell; heavy, distinct, evenly spaced growth rings

HABITAT: brackish to freshwater; rivers, lakes, streams, canals, reservoirs; on silt, sand, gravel-bottomed areas or slightly buried; prefers moving water with high oxygen levels; no tolerance for polluted or near-freezing water

ORIGIN: native to Southeast Asia; first discovered in 1938 in Washington; intentionally introduced as a food item for humans and possibly released; by the 1970s, found its way into most of the Mississippi River Basin

SPREAD BY: primarily human activities, including fishing (on/in equipment); bait bucket releases; aquaculture; mixed in with sand and gravel for construction; movement on its own via water currents

HOW YOU CAN HELP:

Your boat and trailer could possibly be contaminated with adults or free-floating larvae. In addition, be sure to check your waders, hip boots, clothing and all fishing/scuba gear.

- **CLEAN • DRAIN • DRY** (page 20)
- **REPORT** new sightings to your state's natural resource agency (page 124); note date, exact location (page 128) and include a photograph, if possible
- Place specimen in a sealed plastic bag (or in rubbing alcohol) and report

Many are hermaphroditic, an excellent way to reproduce rapidly.

IMPACT ON YOU!

Chinese mitten crabs can interfere with fishing by stealing bait. Their mass migrations often destroy the nets and lines of shrimpers and other fishermen.

- Blocks or clogs traps, nets, water-intake pipes
- Hosts Oriental lung fluke, a human health concern
- Eats almost anything—including aquatic plants, native fish eggs, mollusks and shellfish

For more information go to www.usgs.gov or scan this code with your smart phone. See page 31 for details.

Chinese mitten crab

Eriocheir sinensis

OTHER COMMON NAMES: Shanghai hairy crab, big binding crab, big sluice crab

DESCRIPTION: body up to 4 inches wide; light brown to olive green; "furry" claws (look like mittens) with white tips; 8 sharp-tipped walking legs are more than twice as long as body width

HABITAT: shallow waters in bays and estuaries; migrates upstream in rivers and streams; spends most of its life in freshwater, returning to salt water to spawn

ORIGIN: native to northern China and Korea; probably introduced via **ballast** water; first reported in the Great Lakes in 1965 when a specimen was caught in a water-intake pipe; several found migrating in Thunder Bay, Lake Superior, in 2005 and 2007

SPREAD BY: recreational and commercial boating activities; deliberate release by humans; can survive for days out of water and migrates overland to new areas on its own; a single female can produce from 250,000 to more than 1 million eggs

 HOW YOU CAN HELP:

The best control is preventing their spread. Once established, Chinese mitten crabs have the ability to disperse widely and quickly on their own.

- **CLEAN • DRAIN • DRY** page 20
- **REPORT** new sightings to your state's natural resource agency (page 124); note date, exact location (page 128) and include a photograph, if possible
- If you catch a Chinese mitten crab—**do not release it!**
- Keep the entire carcass (freeze if necessary) and report

These crabs crawl easily on land and can readily bypass most obstructions during their migrations.

IMPACT ON YOU!

Red swamp crayfish can be a host for parasites and diseases and can carry crayfish fungus plague.

- Once established, can affect an ecosystem due to its diverse diet, including plants, insects, snails, fish and amphibians
- Aggressively competes with native crayfish and other species for food and habitat

For more information go to www.usgs.gov or scan this code with your smart phone. See page 31 for details.

Red swamp crayfish
Procambarus clarkii

OTHER COMMON NAMES: Louisiana crayfish, Louisiana lobster, American crayfish, red swamp crawfish

DESCRIPTION: up to 5 inches (with claws); dark red body and claws with spiky, bright red bumps; black wedge-shaped stripe on underside; females can burrow

HABITAT: flowing to non-flowing freshwater, salt water; permanent ponds; areas of streams and ditches with organic debris; agricultural areas; wetlands; builds chimney-like burrows

ORIGIN: native to the Gulf Coast and the Mississippi River drainage to Illinois; probably introduced through **aquaculture**, as it is a popular food worldwide

SPREAD BY: bait bucket release by anglers; being used for culinary purposes; released study specimens; accidental release from live-food trade; can walk several miles overland to a new pond

HOW YOU CAN HELP:

Know your state's regulations. Your help is needed to detect new infestations and prevent their spread. Be on the lookout while in the field and don't use them as bait.

- **CLEAN • DRAIN • DRY** page 20
- **REPORT** new sightings to your state's natural resource agency (page 124); note date, exact location (page 128) and include a photograph, if possible
- If you catch a red swamp crayfish—**do not release it!**
- Keep the entire carcass (freeze if necessary) and report

Prized as one of the traditional culinary dishes of New Orleans!

IMPACT ON YOU!

Rusty crayfish eliminate vegetation that provides cover for fish and habitat for invertebrates, an important food for fish and waterfowl. They also can harm native fish populations by eating their eggs and young.

- Competes aggressively with native crayfish for food . . . can eat up to twice as much
- Can **hybridize** with native crayfish

For more information go to www.usgs.gov or scan this code with your smart phone. See page 31 for details.

Rusty crayfish
Orconectes rusticus

OTHER COMMON NAMES: rusty crawfish, rusty crawdads, rusties

DESCRIPTION: up to 6 inches (with claws); brown body; males often
with dark rusty spots on each side (as though you picked it
up with paint on your fingers); large, smooth grayish-green to
reddish-brown claws with a black band at the tips, claws have an
oval gap when closed; "S"-shaped movable claw

HABITAT: lakes, ponds, rivers, streams; bottom areas with rocks,
logs or other debris for cover; needs permanent water

ORIGIN: native to Ohio River Basin; first discovered in 1960s in
Wisconsin and Minnesota

SPREAD BY: likely bait bucket releases by anglers; home aquarium
releases; study specimen release; females with stored sperm
may be able to establish new populations

HOW YOU CAN HELP:

The best method to control rusty crayfish is to prevent new
introductions, as eradicating established infestations is impossible.
Do not use as bait outside the Ohio River drainage.

- **CLEAN • DRAIN • DRY** page 20
- **REPORT** your catch or new sightings to your state's
  natural resource agency (page 124); note date, exact
  location (page 128) and include a photograph, if possible
- If you catch a rusty crayfish—**do not release it!**
- Keep the entire carcass (freeze if necessary) and report

*When threatened, it often takes an aggressive defensive posture
with claws raised, so not eaten as often as native crayfish.*

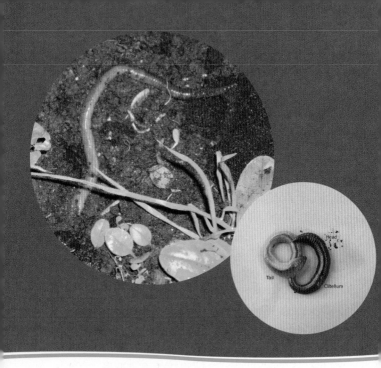

IMPACT ON YOU!

Earthworms can alter the soil chemistry and biology of the forest floor such that native plants and trees have difficulty establishing roots in the compacted soil.

- Removal of leaf litter eliminates critical habitat for invertebrates that provide food for small mammals and forest-dwelling birds

For more information go to www.usgs.gov or scan this code with your smart phone. See page 31 for details.

Common earthworm
Lumbricus terrestris

OTHER COMMON NAMES: night crawler, dew worm, green crawler, large crawler, nitro crawler, angleworm

DESCRIPTION: up to 10 inches; pinkish to reddish-brown; distinct, darker colored "head" end; "tail" end more flattened and lighter in color

HABITAT: moist soils that are rich in organic matter; deep vertical burrows of 6½ feet or more; forested lands along major waterways; land altered by human activity

ORIGIN: the last ice age in the Great Lakes eliminated all native earthworms in the Northeast forest; native to Eurasia; probably first arrived in soils, either used for ship **ballast** or in potted plants

SPREAD BY: primarily anglers dumping bait; use in gardens; unintentional transport in plant material and soil; **hermaphroditic**, allowing a new population to form from just a few individuals

HOW YOU CAN HELP:

Place unwanted bait in the trash. It's illegal to release most non-native species into the wild.

• **CLEAN** • **DRAIN** • **DRY** page 20

Earthworms act as soil engineers, creating new conditions favorable to invasive species.

IMPACT ON YOU!

As an invader in South America, the golden mussel has caused significant problems. Its impact has been similar to the impacts of the zebra mussel (page 53) and quagga mussel (page 51) in our region. In addition, the golden mussel can survive in a wider range of habitats than either the zebra mussel or the quagga mussel.

For more information go to www.usgs.gov or scan this code with your smart phone. See page 31 for details.

Golden mussel
Limnoperna fortunei

OTHER COMMON NAMES: none

DESCRIPTION: ranges from just under ½ inch to 2 inches; distinctive golden or yellowish shell; inner surface has a purple mother-of-pearl layer

HABITAT: **brackish** to freshwater; lakes, rivers, estuaries, wetlands, bodies of water in urban areas; attaches to hard surfaces by means of **byssal threads**; capable of colonizing in water temperatures as far north as the lower Great Lakes region

ORIGIN: native to China and Southeast Asia; likely introduced into South America through **ballast** water; not yet detected in North America, but predicted to be a future ballast water threat

SPREAD BY: recreationists transporting mussels attached to aquatic plants, boats, nets, fishing equipment and microscopic larvae in the water

 HOW YOU CAN HELP:

As a species of concern that is not established in the United States, the golden mussel provides an example of why we must increase efforts in prevention, early detection and rapid response to new introductions. Learn how to recognize golden mussels.

- **CLEAN • DRAIN • DRY** page 20
- **REPORT** new sightings to your state's natural resource agency (page 124); note date, exact location (page 128) and include a photograph, if possible
- Place specimen in a sealed plastic bag (or in rubbing alcohol) and report

Like zebra and quagga mussel invaders, their microscopic larvae disperse widely before they settle and grow.

IMPACT ON YOU!

Extensive mats of quagga mussels filter **plankton** from the water, altering the **food web** from the bottom up, ultimately threatening commercial/sport fishing in the Great Lakes.

- Colonizes soft and hard substrates covering fish spawning areas
- Colonizes docks; pollutes swimming areas with sharp shells
- Linked to fish/wildlife die-offs due to **botulism**

For more information go to www.usgs.gov or scan this code with your smart phone. See page 31 for details.

Quagga mussel
Dreissena bugensis

OTHER COMMON NAMES: none

DESCRIPTION: thumbnail-size, laterally compressed shell is pale colored or has alternating brown to brownish stripes; pale near **hinge**

COMPARE: topples over if you try to set it on its ventral (lower) surface; zebra mussels (page 53) can sit flat and are "D" shaped

HABITAT: surfaces (rocks, boats, docks, etc.) from shallow to deep water in lakes, rivers, canals, ponds; more tolerant of deeper and cooler water than their zebra mussel cousin; blankets soft-bottomed areas to depths of 400 feet

ORIGIN: native to Eurasia; first discovered in Lake Erie in 1989; likely transported via **ballast** water; now in parts of all Great Lakes

SPREAD BY: attaches to boats, motors, lifts, aquatic plants; can reproduce in water near freezing; microscopic **veligers** (larvae) can be present in bait buckets and livewells even in late fall or early winter

 HOW YOU CAN HELP:

The primary way quagga mussels spread to inland waters is on trailered boats. It is critical to inspect and remove all plants, animals and mud before leaving the water access area.

- **CLEAN • DRAIN • DRY** page 20
- **REPORT** new sightings to your state's natural resource agency (page 124); note date, exact location (page 128) and include a photograph, if possible
- Place specimen in a sealed plastic bag (or in rubbing alcohol) and report

In areas of the Great Lakes, they are displacing zebra mussels.

IMPACT ON YOU!

Zebra mussels are a serious problem and can encrust boat hulls, piers and moorings. Larvae drawn into boat engine intakes can colonize the interiors of engine cooling systems.

- Disrupts aquatic food web
- Facilitates nuisance plant growth
- Sharp shells littering beaches can make a stroll hazardous
- Smothers native clams/mussels (many are rare) and crayfish

For more information go to www.usgs.gov or scan this code with your smart phone. See page 31 for details.

Zebra mussel
Dreissena polymorpha

OTHER COMMON NAMES: none

DESCRIPTION: under 1 inch (up to 2); black to brownish "D"-shaped shell, generally with alternating dark and light stripes (zebra-like); usually in clusters of individuals; on smooth surfaces, young feel like fine sandpaper, juveniles are peppercorn-size

COMPARE: zebra mussels can sit flat on their ventral (lower) surface, quagga mussels (page 51) cannot

HABITAT: attaches to hard surfaces (rocks, logs, boats, docks, etc.); generally in shallow (6–30 feet) algae-rich water of lakes, rivers, canals, ponds

ORIGIN: native to Eastern Europe; introduced to Great Lakes in late 1980s by **ballast** water; spread to the Mississippi River, its tributaries and inland lakes

SPREAD BY: recreationists transporting mussels attached to aquatic plants, boats, nets, fishing equipment and in water; produces several hundred thousand microscopic eggs per season

 HOW YOU CAN HELP:

Zebra mussels are now found in all the Great Lakes and many U.S. states. The cost of prevention and control is estimated to exceed $500 million annually.

- **CLEAN • DRAIN • DRY** page 20
- **REPORT** new sightings to your state's natural resource agency (page 124); note date, exact location (page 128) and include a photograph, if possible
- Place specimen in a sealed plastic bag (or in rubbing alcohol) and report

Strains the microscopic food of fish larvae (up to 1 quart water per mussel per day), making water clearer . . . but less productive! **53**

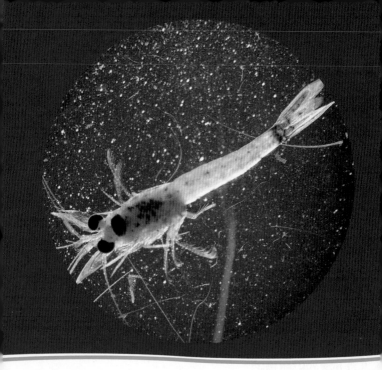

IMPACT ON YOU!

Based on its history of invasion in Europe, bloody red shrimp may significantly impact native fisheries; they have a huge appetite for the **zooplankton** that small fish eat.

- Poses a high risk to harm fish populations through food web impacts.

For more information go to www.usgs.gov or scan this code with your smart phone. See page 31 for details.

Bloody red shrimp
Hemimysis anomala

OTHER COMMON NAMES: red mysid, red mysis, *Hemimysis*

DESCRIPTION: under ½ inch; bright red to orange-red; black eyes on stalks

HABITAT: prefers slow-moving waters; rocky, wave-exposed shorelines; shaded areas of piers or docks or rocky bottoms; avoids direct sunlight; free-swimming when not resting

ORIGIN: native to Eastern Europe, the same area zebra mussels (page 53) came from; most likely introduced to the Great Lakes in **ballast** water; first identified in Lake Michigan in 2006 and since spread to other Great Lakes

SPREAD BY: ballast water; range expansion

 HOW YOU CAN HELP:

Bloody red shrimp are considered a "high risk" species for invasion of inland lakes.

- **CLEAN • DRAIN • DRY** page 20
- **REPORT** new sightings to your state's natural resource agency (page 124); note date, exact location (page 128) and include a photograph, if possible
- Do not transport living specimens
- Place specimens in a glass/plastic container filled with ethanol (grain alcohol) or rubbing alcohol and report

In daytime, these shrimp often form reddish "clouds" in the shadows of piers, boats or breakwalls.

IMPACT ON YOU!

When they invade largemouth bass nests, banded mystery snails significantly reduce the survival of bass eggs.

- Competes with native snails for food and habitat
- Serves as a host for parasites that may be transmitted to fish and other wildlife

For more information go to www.usgs.gov or scan this code with your smart phone. See page 31 for details.

IMPACT ON YOU!

Chinese mystery snails may transmit parasites and diseases. They can also clog the screens of water-intake pipes.

- Achieves very high densities and adversely affects aquatic **food webs**
- Competes with native snails for food and may contribute to their decline (many are already rare)

For more information go to www.usgs.gov or scan this code with your smart phone. See page 31 for details.

Banded mystery snail
Viviparus georgianus

OTHER COMMON NAMES: mystery snail, banded apple snail, pond snail

DESCRIPTION: large (up to 1¾ inches); olive-green shell has 4–5 **whorls** with distinct **sutures**; 4 reddish bands circle the shell (sometimes only visible from the inside); along the **lip** of the shell, there are ridges and "hairs" with hooked ends

HABITAT: sandy-bottomed areas of lakes, ponds, slow-moving rivers, streams

ORIGIN: native the northeast to Florida, Gulf of Mexico, Mississippi River to Illinois; introduced intentionally into the Hudson River by an amateur **conchologist** in 1867; spread to the Great Lakes via the Erie Canal and Mohawk River

SPREAD BY: release from home aquariums; transport by boats and equipment

👉 HOW YOU CAN HELP:

The best way to control banded mystery snails is to prevent them from spreading. They are illegal to release into the wild in some states. Know your state's laws.

- **CLEAN • DRAIN • DRY** page 20
- **REPORT** new sightings to your state's natural resource agency (page 124); note date, exact location (page 128) and include a photograph, if possible
- Place specimen in a sealed plastic bag (or in rubbing alcohol) and report

Called "mystery snails" because in spring, they give birth to fully developed young snails that suddenly and mysteriously appear!

Chinese mystery snail

Cipangopaludina chinensis malleata

OTHER COMMON NAMES: Oriental mystery snail, Asian apple snail, Chinese vivipara, rice snail, Japanese mystery snail, black snail, trapdoor snail

DESCRIPTION: large (up to 2¼ inches); light brownish to olive green shell has 6–7 tightly wound **whorls** without banding; very fine growth rings; a round or oval black **lip**; camouflages itself with a dark green covering similar to moss

HABITAT: shallow, quiet waters of ponds, marshes, lakes, canals, ditches and slow-moving rivers; on vegetation or soft, muddy and sandy-bottomed areas

ORIGIN: native to eastern Asia; sold in Chinese food markets in San Francisco in the late 1800s; by 1965, established on both coasts; introduced into Great Lakes in 1940s

SPREAD BY: release from live-food markets and home aquariums

HOW YOU CAN HELP:

The best way to control Chinese mystery snails is to prevent them from spreading. They are illegal to release into the wild in some states. Know your state's laws.

- **CLEAN • DRAIN • DRY** page 20
- **REPORT** new sightings to your state's natural resource agency (page 124); note date, exact location (page 128) and include a photograph, if possible
- Place specimen in a sealed plastic bag (or in rubbing alcohol) and report

A "trapdoor" feature allows it to close its shell opening when conditions are unfavorable, hampering chemical efforts to eradicate it.

IMPACT ON YOU!

Faucet snails are hosts to parasites, called trematodes, that are linked to the deaths of tens of thousands of diving ducks, such as scaups and coots, in Minnesota and Wisconsin.

- Carriers of additional parasites that affect fish and waterfowl
- Becomes overabundant and fouls surfaces
- Infests municipal water supplies

For more information go to www.usgs.gov or scan this code with your smart phone. See page 31 for details.

Faucet snail
Bithynia tentaculata

OTHER COMMON NAMES: mud bithynia, common bithynia

DESCRIPTION: up to ½ inch; shiny, pale brown shell with 4–5 **whorls**; opening is on the right when shell is pointed up; thick **lip**; able to close **aperture** with an **operculum**

HABITAT: freshwater ponds, river and lake bottoms, canals, vegetated rocky shorelines; docks, attached to other objects in the water; prefers stable water levels; migrates to muddy zone in fall

ORIGIN: native to Europe; introduced to Great Lakes in 1870s; most likely in **ballast** water or vegetation used in packing crates; now established in several Great Lakes and spreading down the Mississippi River

SPREAD BY: hitchhiking on boats, trailers, fishing/hunting equipment, aquatic plants, mud; in the water of bait buckets, livewells, bilges

👉 HOW YOU CAN HELP:

Many bodies of water are regulated as infested waters to prevent the spread of faucet snails to new locations. In some states, it is illegal to transport infested water on a public road. Know the rules.

- **CLEAN • DRAIN • DRY** page 20
- **REPORT** new sightings to your state's natural resource agency (page 124); note date, exact location (page 128) and include a photograph, if possible
- Examine anchors, ropes, push poles, waterfowl decoys
- Place specimen in a sealed plastic bag (or in rubbing alcohol) and report

May reproduce continuously from spring to fall.

IMPACT ON YOU!

New Zealand mudsnails may affect critical **food webs** in trout streams and other waters. They also may compete for food with native bottom-dwellers.

- Lacks predators and reproduces at an alarmingly high rate
- Colonizes quickly; can reach densities of 500,000 individuals per square meter!

For more information go to www.usgs.gov or scan this code with your smart phone. See page 31 for details.

New Zealand mudsnail
Potamopyrgus antipodarum

OTHER COMMON NAMES: Jenkin's spire shell, pond snail, mudsnail

DESCRIPTION: very tiny, up to ³/₁₆ inch; dark gray, light to dark brown shell; cone-shaped with 7–8 right-handed **whorls**, separated by deep grooves; possesses an **operculum**

COMPARE: difficult to distinguish from native snails, but shell more elongate

HABITAT: from flowing freshwater with silt/sand sediment to very **brackish** rivers; lives in water as deep as 60 feet in freshwater lakes and reservoirs

ORIGIN: native to New Zealand; found in Idaho in 1987, introduced with stocked rainbow trout; established in Lake Ontario in 1991; spreading in the Great Lakes

SPREAD BY: clings to anything from floating leaves to wading anglers; can reproduce by **parthenogenesis,** which allows them to spread easily

HOW YOU CAN HELP:

Anglers pose a risk for spread because snails can easily be moved on felt-soled waders or fishing gear.

- **CLEAN • DRAIN • DRY** page 20
- **REPORT** new sightings to your state's natural resource agency (page 124); note date, exact location (page 128) and include a photograph, if possible
- Place specimen in a sealed plastic bag (or in rubbing alcohol) and report

New Zealand mudsnails can survive out of water for days!

Fishing line with clump of fishhook waterfleas

Individual fishhook waterflea enlarged
1,000 times

Fishing net covered with fishhook waterfleas

IMPACT ON YOU!

The fishhook waterflea's "hook" catches on fishing lines and nets,
fouling gear and lowering the quality of recreational fishing and
charter trips.

- Jams the first eyelet of fishing rods, often resulting in the loss
  of a hooked fish
- Devours **plankton**, essential to the diet of larval native fish
- Can coat commercial fishing nets

For more information go to www.usgs.gov or scan this code
with your smart phone. See page 31 for details.

Fishhook waterflea
Cercopagis pengoi

OTHER COMMON NAMES: fish-hook water flea

DESCRIPTION: ¼–⅝ inch; long tail spine ending in a "hook"; prominent dark eyespot; can form clumps (with black spots) that look and feel like gelatin or wet cotton

HABITAT: **brackish** to freshwater; deep lakes, shallow water bodies

ORIGIN: native to Northern Europe; reported in Lake Ontario in 1998, likely introduced in **ballast** water; spread to Lakes Michigan and Erie

SPREAD BY: angling and boating equipment; eggs can be transported between lakes in early spring in sediment stuck to anchors and downrigger cables

 HOW YOU CAN HELP:

Anglers often discover new infestations. Fishhook waterfleas can accumulate on gear and spread when that gear is used in a new body of water.

- **CLEAN • DRAIN • DRY** page 20
- **REPORT** new sightings to your state's natural resource agency (page 124); note date, exact location (page 128) and include a photograph, if possible
- Do not transport waterfleas alive; preserve them in ethanol (grain alcohol) or rubbing alcohol
- Drain water from specimens; place in alcohol-filled glass or plastic container and report
- Remove gelatinous blobs or cotton-like material from gear (to do this, pluck the line like a guitar string)
- Examine line at swivel, lure and downrigger connections, and inspect nets and anchor ropes

New populations can even start from eggs in dead females.

Fishing line with clump of spiny waterfleas

Individual spiny waterflea enlarged 1,000 times

IMPACT ON YOU!

Spiny waterfleas collect on fishing gear, especially lines and downrigger cables, lowering the quality of recreational fishing and charter trips.

- Jams the first eyelet of fishing rods, often resulting in the loss of a hooked fish
- Clumps can damage the drag on some reels
- Disrupts **food web** of the aquatic **ecosystem**

For more information go to www.usgs.gov or scan this code with your smart phone. See page 31 for details.

Spiny waterflea

Bythotrephes longimanus

OTHER COMMON NAMES: Eurasian spiny waterflea

DESCRIPTION: tiny (½ inch) and translucent with a long, sharply barbed tail spine; dark eyespot is prominent; large numbers form clumps (with black spots) that look/feel like gelatin or wet cotton

HABITAT: deep lakes, reservoirs, shallow water, large rivers, oxbows

ORIGIN: native to Northern Europe; likely introduced in **ballast** water; discovered in Lake Ontario in 1982; spread to all Great Lakes and some inland lakes

SPREAD BY: angling and boating gear contaminated with adults carrying eggs

 HOW YOU CAN HELP:

Anglers often discover new infestations of spiny waterfleas accumulating on fishing gear. If not removed from all equipment, waterfleas can infest another body of water.

- **CLEAN • DRAIN • DRY** (page 20)
- **REPORT** new sightings to your state's natural resource agency (page 124); note date, exact location (page 128) and include a photograph, if possible
- Do not transport waterfleas alive; preserve them in ethanol (grain alcohol) or rubbing alcohol
- Drain water from specimens; place in alcohol-filled glass or plastic container and report
- Remove gelatinous blobs or cotton-like material from gear (to do this, pluck the line like a guitar string)
- Examine line at swivel, lure and downrigger connections, and inspect fishing nets and anchor ropes

Don't let their small size fool you; spiny waterfleas can have as serious an effect on aquatic food webs as larger invaders!

AQUATIC PLANTS

Aquatic plants can grow nearly anywhere there is water—on the surface of lakes or ponds, at the bottom, along the water's edge, in the flowing water of streams and rivers, or in flooded lands or meadows.

Like all plants, aquatic plants require sunlight to grow and for photosynthesis to occur. Consequently, aquatic plants are more abundant in the shallows as less light penetrates in deeper water.

When it comes to roots, aquatic plants vary. Some aquatic plants have roots in the mud and submersed leaves, while others have roots in the mud and floating leaves. Still others simply float and are not connected to the bottom at all. In fast-moving rivers, many plants have strong roots that keep them securely anchored, while others have stems that move easily in the flow.

Plant Anatomy

Because they are supported by water, the structural needs of aquatic plants are quite simple. The **stem** is the principal shoot of a plant. Nodes are points along a stem from which leaves,

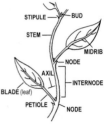

branches or flowers grow. The leaf stalk (petiole) is the small stem that attaches a leaf to the main plant stem. The **leaves**, sometimes made up of many little leaflets, commonly function as the principal organ in photosynthesis.

Plants use a variety of different structures to reproduce. These include rhizomes, stolons, tubers and turions. Each contains everything a plant needs to grow, bloom and complete its life cycle. Each structure works in a different way. **Rhizomes** are essentially underground stems that grow horizontally just below the soil's surface. They feature many growing points for new plants. **Stolons** are horizontal above ground stems that root at several points, forming new plants. A runner is a type of stolon. **Tubers** are located underground and form at the end of roots or on

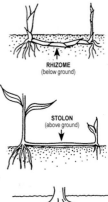

RHIZOME
(below ground)

STOLON
(above ground)

TUBERS

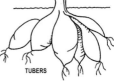

rhizomes; they are small, potato-like or pea-like, usually white or yellowish, and overwinter and sprout in the spring. **Turions** are hardy plant buds that are found along the stem of certain aquatic plants. They detach, drift on currents or fall to the bottom. After overwintering, they grow into a new plant the following spring.

TURION

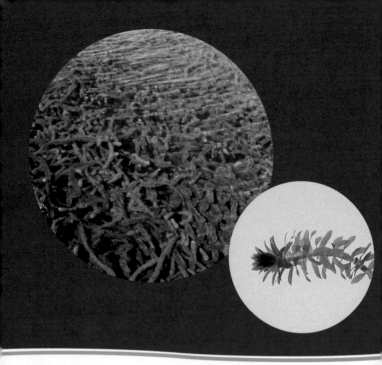

IMPACT ON YOU!

Dense stands of Brazilian elodea can interfere with water-based recreation, such as fishing, boating and swimming, dramatically impacting tourism on infested lakes.

- Crowds out important native aquatic plants
- Degrades fish and waterfowl habitat
- Creates breeding ground for mosquitoes

For more information go to www.usgs.gov or scan this code with your smart phone. See page 31 for details.

IMPACT ON YOU!

European frogbit can blanket shallow ponds, marshes and shorelines. Dense layers of interlocking plants and dangling roots dramatically reduce habitat for game fish, such as pike and bass.

- Interferes with fishing, boating, waterfowl hunting and swimming
- Hinders the movement of fish and waterfowl
- Greatly inhibits the growth of native vegetation

For more information go to www.usgs.gov or scan this code with your smart phone. See page 31 for details.

Brazilian elodea
Egeria densa

OTHER COMMON NAMES: Brazilian waterweed

DESCRIPTION: very bushy; rooted in water (up to 20 feet deep) or drifting in open water; can form dense mats visible at surface; bright green leaves with 4–8 **whorls** that are close together along the **stem** (looks bushy); white flowers are present about 1 inch above the water in spring or early summer

COMPARE: a native look-alike, American elodea (*Elodea canadensis*), has smaller leaves in whorls of 2–3; also confused with Hydrilla (page 77)

HABITAT: slow-moving or still water in lakes, ponds and rivers; streams, ponds, springs, ditches

ORIGIN: native to South America; likely introduced by aquarium releases or accidentally shipped with aquatic plants

SPREAD BY: plant **fragments** easily tangle on boats, boat trailers, motors, equipment, fishing and diving gear

 HOW YOU CAN HELP:

Dispose of unwanted aquarium or water garden plants in the trash. Be sure to rinse plant purchases to remove mud, unwanted plant fragments and other "hitchhikers."

- **CLEAN • DRAIN • DRY** page 20
- **REPORT** new sightings to your state's natural resource agency (page 124); note date, exact location (page 128) and include a photograph, if possible
- Wrap specimen in a wet paper towel, place in sealed plastic bag and report

Can survive periods of unfavorable conditions, such as flooding, and then rapidly spread during more favorable conditions.

European frogbit

Hydrocharis morsus-ranae

OTHER COMMON NAMES: tape-grass, common frog-bit, frog-bit

DESCRIPTION: free-floating; resembles small water lilies; can form impenetrable mats at surface; leaves are heart-shaped, leathery and spongy with purplish red undersides; roots dangle underneath; single, 3-petaled white flower about 1 inch above water

COMPARE: leaf **stem** has no midline groove; native American frogbit (*Limnobium spongia*) has a midline groove but has coarse teeth along leaf edge

HABITAT: quiet, shallow, slow-moving water; edges of lakes, rivers, streams; swamps, marshes, ditches

ORIGIN: escaped from cultivation in Ontario, Canada, in 1932; spread along rivers into the Northeast; in Lakes Michigan and Huron; spreading inland

SPREAD BY: clinging to boats, trailers, equipment; escape from water gardens; "daughter" plants break free and float on currents; **turions** sink in fall and float up in spring to grow into new plants

HOW YOU CAN HELP:

Herbicides can provide some control of European frogbit. Hand-harvesting offers temporary relief near docks and swimming areas.

- **CLEAN • DRAIN • DRY** (page 20)
- **REPORT** new sightings to your state's natural resource agency (page 124); note date, exact location (page 128) and include a photograph, if possible
- Wrap specimen in a wet paper towel, place in sealed plastic bag and report

Boaters, anglers and water gardeners all need to work together to prevent this invader from spreading into new areas.

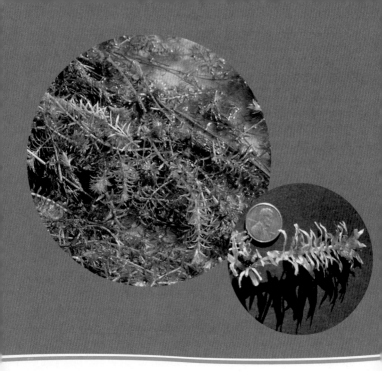

IMPACT ON YOU!

Dense, thick mats can cover vast acres, making water-based recreation difficult. Hydrilla also alters habitat by crowding out native aquatic plants, harming fish and wildlife.

- Hinders fishing, boating and swimming
- Lowers waterfront property values
- Blocks water-delivery systems

For more information go to www.usgs.gov or scan this code with your smart phone. See page 31 for details.

Hydrilla
Hydrilla verticillata

OTHER COMMON NAMES: Florida elodea, water thyme, Wasserquirl, Indian star-vine

DESCRIPTION: long, intertwined stems form dense mats visible at surface; **whorls** of 4–8 pointy leaves with coarse teeth along the edges; small **tubers** at the end of the root; tiny, white, floating flowers present in mid-late summer

COMPARE: native elodea (*Elodea canadensis*) has smaller leaves in whorls of 2–3; easily confused with Brazilian elodea (page 73)

HABITAT: slow-moving or still water in lakes and rivers; tolerates many conditions including low light, drops in water level and high levels of suspended sediment

ORIGIN: native to Africa, Asia and Australia; likely introduced by an aquarium or water garden release or accidentally included in aquatic plant shipments

SPREAD BY: plant pieces tangled on boats, trailers, fishing equipment; overwintering **tubers/turions; fragmentation**

 HOW YOU CAN HELP:

The most troublesome aquatic plant in the United States. As it spreads north, hydrilla costs millions of dollars due to lost tourist revenues and the expense of controlling infestations.

- **CLEAN • DRAIN • DRY** page 20
- **REPORT** new sightings to your state's natural resource agency (page 124); note date, exact location (page 128) and include a photograph, if possible
- Wrap specimen in a wet paper towel, place in sealed plastic bag and report

Grows earlier and faster than most aquatic plants—up to 1 inch per day. Don't use hydrilla in aquariums or water gardens.

IMPACT ON YOU!

Purple loosestrife outcompetes and replaces native grasses, sedges and other flowering plants that provide a higher quality source of cover, food or nesting sites for native wetland fish and wildlife.

- Adapts readily to natural and disturbed wetlands
- Reduces habitat for waterfowl
- Seeds remain viable even after 2–3 years underwater

For more information go to www.usgs.gov or scan this code with your smart phone. See page 31 for details.

Purple loosestrife
Lythrum salicaria

OTHER COMMON NAMES: purple lythrum, spiked loosestrife, salicaire, bouquet violet, rainbow weed

DESCRIPTION: 4–10 feet high; multiple ridged or square woody stems often covered by downy hair; leaves opposite, lance-shaped, stalkless, rounded to heart-shaped at the base; showy magenta-colored flower spikes, individual flowers have 5–7 petals

COMPARE: blue vervain, blazing star, Canada germander, swamp milkweed, fireweed

HABITAT: wet meadows, marshes, river and stream banks, pond edges, reservoirs, ditches; tolerates wide range of conditions; low nutrient requirements

ORIGIN: native to Eurasia; early 1800s for beekeeping, as an ornamental plant and in discarded soil used as **ballast** on ships

SPREAD BY: mud and seeds on vehicle tires, boats, trailers, equipment, clothing; a mature plant produces 2–3 million seeds annually; dispersed by water and wind; underground stems; continues to be promoted as a landscape plant and bee **forage**

 HOW YOU CAN HELP:

On The Nature Conservancy's "Dirty Dozen" list, purple loosestrife causes a loss of about 500,000 acres of wetland habitat each year.

- **CLEAN • DRAIN • DRY** page 20
- **REPORT** new sightings to your state's natural resource agency (page 124); note date, exact location (page 128) and include a photograph, if possible
- Wrap specimen in wet paper towel, place in a sealed plastic bag and report

Has been labeled the "purple plague" because it can devastate natural communities.

IMPACT ON YOU!

Dense beds of curlyleaf pondweed can restrict access to docks and sport fishing areas in spring and early summer. In mid-late summer, decaying piles can cover shorelines and beaches.

- Plant die-offs reduce available oxygen for fish
- The release of nutrients can also trigger harmful **algal blooms**
- Early, rapid growth shades out native aquatic plants

For more information go to www.usgs.gov or scan this code with your smart phone. See page 31 for details.

Curlyleaf pondweed
Potamogeton crispus

OTHER COMMON NAMES: curly leaf pondweed, curly-leaved pondweed, crispy-leaved pondweed

DESCRIPTION: grows to depths of 15 feet; forms thick surface mats; drops to the lake bottom in midsummer; leaves are oblong, reddish-green, and wavy, with fine-toothed edges; stems are flat, reddish-brown and 1–3 feet long

COMPARE: distinguished from other pondweeds by its unique life cycle: often the first species to appear after ice-out; dies back in midsummer

HABITAT: shallow, soft bottoms in clear or polluted lakes, reservoirs, ponds, rivers, streams or springs; tolerates low light and low temperatures

ORIGIN: native to Eurasia, Africa and Australia; accidently introduced in the 1800s in the Northeast by an aquarium release

SPREAD BY: turions and plant fragments on boats, trailers, fishing gear; plantings for wildlife; new plants forming under ice in winter; rhizomes, stem fragments

HOW YOU CAN HELP:

Curlyleaf pondweed is considered "ecologically invasive" in Wisconsin, "highly invasive" in Upper Michigan, and a "prohibited invasive species" in Minnesota.

- **CLEAN • DRAIN • DRY** page 20
- **REPORT** new sightings to your state's natural resource agency (page 124); note date, exact location (page 128) and include a photograph, if possible
- Wrap specimen in wet paper towel, place in a sealed plastic bag and report

The summer "dieback" can lead to fish kills.

IMPACT ON YOU!

Extensive floating mats of water chestnut can make boat navigation, fishing and swimming difficult or impossible. Decaying in the fall, it reduces oxygen levels in the water, increasing the potential for fish kills.

- Inhibits the growth of native aquatic plants
- Its low food value can decrease use of area by waterfowl and other native species

For more information go to www.usgs.gov or scan this code with your smart phone. See page 31 for details.

Water chestnut
Trapa natans

OTHER COMMON NAMES: European water chestnut, water nut, water-caltrop

DESCRIPTION: floating **rosettes** on long cordlike stems; above water leaves are waxy, triangular and toothed, underwater leaves are feathery and paired; leaf stems have a bladderlike swelling; small, white flowers can bloom until frost; fruit is a hard, barbed nut

HABITAT: full sun; quiet, nutrient-rich open and still water; flood canals, rivers, lakes, reservoirs, wetlands; overwinters in frozen lakes and ponds; colonizes shorelines exposed in low water

ORIGIN: native to Southern Europe and Asia; introduced to the United States in 1874 as part of a botanical collection and was released by a gardener into local waters; established in Lake Ontario

SPREAD BY: plant **fragments** on boats, trailers and fishing gear; rosettes floating to new areas; 1 acre can produce seeds (nuts) to cover 100 acres the following year; nuts can be viable for 12 years

 HOW YOU CAN HELP:

It costs millions of dollars per year to control water chestnut. Detecting and reporting new infestations is vital to prevent them from spreading.

- **CLEAN • DRAIN • DRY** page 20
- **REPORT** new sightings to your state's natural resource agency (page 124); note date, exact location (page 128) and include a photograph, if possible
- Wrap specimen in a wet paper towel, place in sealed plastic bag and report

Nuts have barbed spines sharp enough to penetrate shoe leather and large enough to keep people off beaches.

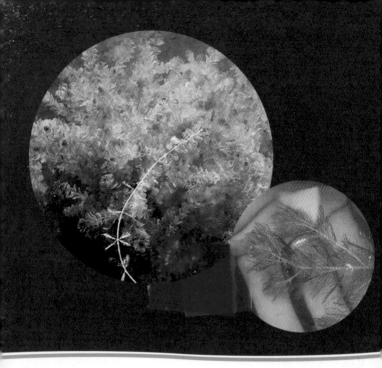

IMPACT ON YOU!

Infestations of Eurasian watermilfoil essentially take over shallow areas of lakes and can interfere with swimming, fishing, waterfowl hunting, and even boating, as plant **fragments** tangle on propellers.

- Can crowd out important native aquatic plants for waterfowl
- Impairs ability of some fish to spawn
- Reduces local property values
- Creates breeding grounds for mosquitoes

For more information go to www.usgs.gov or scan this code with your smart phone. See page 31 for details.

Eurasian watermilfoil
Myriophyllum spicatum

OTHER COMMON NAMES: spike, spiked watermilfoil

DESCRIPTION: submerged, feathery; long stems branch near surface, forming thick mats in shallow water; green leaves with 12–21 threadlike leaflet pairs; 3–5 feathery leaves in **whorls** around the **stem**; small, reddish flowers above water midsummer

COMPARE: the leaf of the native look-alike, northern watermilfoil (*Myriophyllum sibiricum*) has only 5–10 leaflet pairs

HABITAT: shallow freshwater less than 20 feet deep; highly disturbed lakebeds; heavily used lakes and ponds; nutrient-rich areas; ponds; slow-moving areas of rivers and streams

ORIGIN: native to Eurasia and North Africa; accidentally introduced in the 1940s (possibly as early as the 1800s), most likely as a released aquarium plant

SPREAD BY: fragmentation; clinging to boats, trailers, motors, personal watercraft, fishing and diving gear; fragments break off and float with water currents; mechanical clearing can create thousands of fragments

HOW YOU CAN HELP:

Eradicating established infestations is nearly impossible, so detecting and reporting new infestations is vital.

- **CLEAN • DRAIN • DRY** page 20
- **REPORT** new sightings to your state's natural resource agency (page 124); note date, exact location (page 128) and include a photograph, if possible
- Wrap specimen in a wet paper towel, place in a sealed plastic bag and report

Threadlike pairs of leaflets resemble bones on a fish spine.

FISH

About 70 percent of the Earth's surface is covered by salt-water or freshwater. The oldest group of vertebrate—fish—can be found wherever there is water. The Great Lakes alone contain 20 percent of the world's freshwater!

Fish come in all shapes and sizes. There are flat fish, skinny fish, fish that crawl on land, flying fish and even electric fish. Some species have stripes and spots, and fish come in all the colors of the rainbow. The tremendous diversity among fish is the result of 400 million years of adaptation and the unique conditions associated with life in the water.

Parts of a Fish

As fish are specially adapted to life in the water, they have permanent gills, and most have fins and scales. **Gills** are thin membranes located inside slit-like openings behind the head. Fish get oxygen from the water by pulling it through their mouths and over their gills. **Fins** help a fish to balance and move in the water, and each fin has a particular function. The **pectoral fins** are paired, with one on each side behind the gills, and they are used for many different things. In general, they help with diving, swimming to the surface and remaining stationary in the water. There is also a **pelvic, or ventral, fin** on each side for stability. Some fish even adapt these fins for

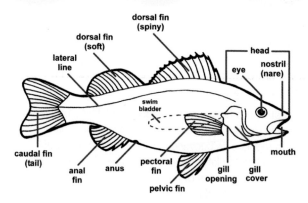

dorsal fin
(spiny)

dorsal fin
(soft)

lateral
line

head

eye

nostril
(nare)

swim
bladder

mouth

caudal fin
(tail)

anal
fin

anus

pectoral
fin

gill
opening

gill
cover

pelvic fin

"walking" or for anchoring to the bottom. The **dorsal fin** stands up from the back and is used to keep the fish from rolling. Some fish have more than one and can have sharp spines for protection against predators. The **anal fin**, located near the rear of the belly, plays an important role in stability and balance. The shape of the tail or **caudal fin** defines the power behind the movement of most fish. A forked tail increases speed, while a broad tail increases maneuverability.

Most fish have protective scales that cover their bodies and serve as armor. Scales, which vary in size and shape, are coated with a slimy layer of mucous that has antiseptic properties, protecting the fish against disease and parasites.

Almost all fish have a **swim bladder**, which is a balloon-like organ in the gut area. The swim bladder helps the fish to regulate its buoyancy. Fish also have a row of pores, called the **lateral line**, in their skin. The pores are connected to a series of nerves, which are very sensitive to vibration. The lateral line extends along the body from just behind the head all the way to the tail on either side of the fish. It can detect even slight vibrations in water, helping the fish to avoid danger or assisting in capturing prey.

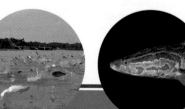

IMPACT ON YOU!

May compete with many native fish species or eat their eggs and larvae; a major prey species of trout, salmon and other game fish.

- Eats **zooplankton**, competing with young native fish
- A commonly consumed prey of lake trout; however a diet high in alewives lowers reproductive success and survival of their fry

For more information go to www.usgs.gov or scan this code with your smart phone. See page 31 for details.

Alewife
Alosa pseudoharengus

OTHER COMMON NAMES: sawbelly, green-back, mooneye, freshwater herring, grayback

DESCRIPTION: 6–7 inches; metallic, silvery-green body; lower jaw rises steeply; black spot behind large eye; scales in a row along belly, hence the name "sawbelly"

COMPARE: native gizzard shad *(Dorosoma cepedianum)* have a **dorsal fin** thread; also very similar to blueback herring (page 105); an alewife has an upturned mouth while a gizzard shad's is downturned

HABITAT: landlocked; spawns in bays and tributaries in late spring; moves offshore in dense schools until late fall; found near bottom until spring

ORIGIN: native to Atlantic Coast; observed in Lake Ontario in 1870s; entered remaining Great Lakes after 1931 via **Welland Canal**; grew to peak abundance in 1950s as populations of lake trout, the lakes' top predator, had declined dramatically

SPREAD BY: accidental bait release by anglers; stocking inland lakes as food for sport fish

 HOW YOU CAN HELP:

To prevent the spread of alewives, do not use them as bait outside the Great Lakes.

- **CLEAN • DRAIN • DRY** page 20
- **REPORT** new inland sightings to your state's natural resource agency (page 124); note date, exact location (page 128) and include a photograph, if possible
- Freeze specimen (or preserve in rubbing alcohol) and report

Spawning stress causes spring die-offs, covering beaches with dead and dying fish, reducing recreational use.

IMPACT ON YOU!

Bighead carp consume 5–20 percent of their body weight daily, competing for food with larvae of native fish, paddlefish and bigmouth buffalo in the upper Mississippi River system.

- Can load the nets of commercial fishermen to the point they are forced to abandon the fishing spot
- Each female produces millions of eggs annually and can live more than 30 years

For more information go to www.usgs.gov or scan this code with your smart phone. See page 31 for details.

Bighead carp

Hypophthalmichthys nobilis

OTHER COMMON NAMES: Asian carp, noble fish, lake fish

DESCRIPTION: up to 60 inches, 130 pounds; dark gray dorsally, paling to silver-white sides with scattered dark blotches; big scaleless head with upturned mouth, no **barbels**; eyes set forward below the midline of body, eyes look downward

COMPARE: similar in appearance to silver carp (page 99) but has dark blotches on body

HABITAT: backwaters of large rivers, lakes and ponds; spawns in flowing water

ORIGIN: native to China; introduced to Arkansas in 1972 for water quality management in fish culture ponds; flooding resulted in its escape (as it did for the silver and black carp) into the Mississippi River Basin

SPREAD BY: range expansion via connected waterways and flooding; possible bait bucket transfers as young carp resemble shad; intentional releases

HOW YOU CAN HELP:

In March 2011, the U.S. Fish and Wildlife Service included bighead carp on the list of injurious fish species.

- **CLEAN • DRAIN • DRY** page 20
- **REPORT** sightings in new areas *immediately* to your state's natural resource agency (page 124)
- Note date, exact location (page 128) and include a photograph, if possible
- Freeze specimen (or preserve in rubbing alcohol) and report

Bigheads grow rapidly; they can gain a pound or more per month.

IMPACT ON YOU!

Black carp stay near or on the bottom and feed heavily on snails and mussels, posing a risk to native mollusks, many of which are endangered or threatened.

- Life span exceeds 15 years; even sterile black carp in the wild have the potential for harm

For more information go to www.usgs.gov or scan this code with your smart phone. See page 31 for details.

Black carp
Mylopharyngodon piceus

OTHER COMMON NAMES: Asian carp, snail carp, Chinese black carp, black amur, Chinese roach, black Chinese roach

DESCRIPTION: up to 60 inches, 150 pounds; blackish brown to dark olive with a white belly, blackish gray **fins**; broad, blunt head, slightly downturned mouth, no **barbels**; no **keel**; large "chain-link" scales

HABITAT: large rivers, lakes and ponds

ORIGIN: native to Eastern Asia; imported for snail control in catfish farms in early 1970s; escaped in Missouri in 1994 when holding ponds flooded; black carp still are used by fish farmers to control snails that host a catfish parasite

SPREAD BY: flooding of fish farms; mistakenly included in grass carp (page 97) introductions; inclusion in bait shipments

HOW YOU CAN HELP:

Although not officially established in the United States, many fishermen from the Gulf Coast to Illinois and Missouri have reported catching them.

- **CLEAN • DRAIN • DRY** page 20
- **REPORT** new sightings to your state's natural resource agency (page 124); note date, exact location (page 128) and include a photograph, if possible
- Freeze specimen (or preserve in rubbing alcohol) and report

Because they eat a lot and reproduce rapidly, they're called "river rabbits" in Australia.

IMPACT ON YOU!

Grass carp are widely established. In large numbers, they can potentially reduce native fish and waterfowl populations and adversely affect their habitat.

- Eliminates vast areas of aquatic plants that are important fish spawning and nursery habitat
- Consumes important aquatic **forage** for waterfowl

For more information go to www.usgs.gov or scan this code with your smart phone. See page 31 for details.

Grass carp
Ctenopharyngodon idella

OTHER COMMON NAMES: Asian carp, white amur

DESCRIPTION: large (up to 49 inches, 99 pounds); silvery dark gray, sides with gold sheen, white belly; broad blunt head, slight downturned mouth, no **barbels**; no **keel**; pointed **dorsal fin** with 8–10 soft rays; large "chain-link" scales

HABITAT: large standing or slow-flowing water with vegetation; lakes, ponds, pools, backwaters of large rivers; tolerates temperatures from freezing to over 100°F, as well as low oxygen levels and **brackish** water

ORIGIN: native to Eastern Asia; introduced in the United States in 1963 to control aquatic plants in fish farms and escaped due to flooding; escapees from stocking by federal and state agencies contributed to their rapid range expansion

SPREAD BY: legal stocking of fertile and sterile fish occurs in many states; escape from stocking locations, natural reproduction

HOW YOU CAN HELP:

Grass carp can now be found in 45 states. If you catch one from a body of water where it was not stocked, do not release the fish alive.

- **CLEAN • DRAIN • DRY** page 20
- **REPORT** new sightings to your state's natural resource agency (page 124); note date, exact location (page 128) and include a photograph, if possible
- Freeze specimen (or preserve in rubbing alcohol) and report

Can eat up to 100 percent of its body weight per day in aquatic plants and live up to 21 years.

IMPACT ON YOU!

Silver carp leap in response to the noise and vibration of boat motors, posing a threat of serious injury to anglers and boaters.

- Can reach high densities following invasion, often dominating fish communities
- Feeds mostly on **plankton**, reducing food for larval fish and **filter-feeding** fish, such as native paddlefish

For more information go to www.usgs.gov or scan this code with your smart phone. See page 31 for details.

Silver carp
Hypophthalmichthys molitrix

OTHER COMMON NAMES: Asian carp, Asian leaping carp, flying carp, silver fin

DESCRIPTION: large (up to 41 inches, 60 lb.); olive green dorsally with bright silver sides; scaleless head, large upturned mouth, no **barbels**; eyes set forward below the midline of body, looking downward; sharp ventral **keel** from **anal fin** to throat; known for its leaping prowess (up to 10 feet out of the water)

COMPARE: similar in appearance to bighead carp (page 93), but lacks the dark blotches on body

HABITAT: near the surface of calm, slow-moving waters; lakes and backwaters of large rivers

ORIGIN: native to Eastern Asia; introduced in 1973 in Arkansas with bighead carp shipments; like bighead carp (page 93) and black carp (page 95), accidentally escaped by flooding; now present throughout much of the Mississippi River Basin

SPREAD BY: range expansion; potential bait bucket transfers

 HOW YOU CAN HELP:

Silver carp are a danger to native fish species. They are spreading rapidly in the United States, and they are on the federal list of injurious species.

- **CLEAN • DRAIN • DRY** (page 20)
- **REPORT** sightings in new areas *immediately* to your state's natural resource agency (page 124)
- Note date, exact location (page 128) and include a photograph, if possible
- Freeze specimen (or preserve in rubbing alcohol) and report

In an effort to popularize them as a food in the United States, some restaurants call them "silver fin."

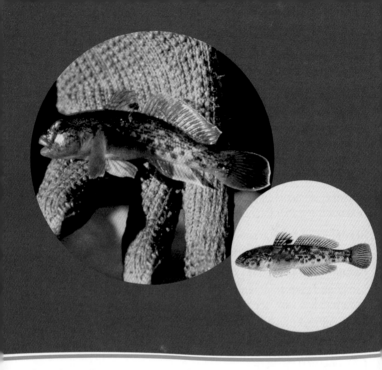

IMPACT ON YOU!

Round gobies eat fish eggs, and may contribute to the decline of sport fish populations, such as smallmouth bass.

- Links in the transfer of **botulism** to waterfowl
- Aggressively competes with native bottom-dwelling fish
- Highly territorial for food, shelter and optimal spawning sites

For more information go to www.usgs.gov or scan this code with your smart phone. See page 31 for details.

Round goby
Neogobius melanostomus

OTHER COMMON NAMES: goby

DESCRIPTION: rarely more than 7 inches long; mottled gray and brown; a single suction cup-like **pelvic fin**; frog-like, bulging eyes; black spot on rear margin of front **dorsal fin**

COMPARE: sculpin appear similar, but these and other native species have paired pelvic fins; the invasive tubenose goby (page 103) also has a single fused pelvic fin

HABITAT: nearshore, rock, cobble or **riprap**; bottom-dwelling; tolerates a wide range of conditions, including low oxygen and polluted waters

ORIGIN: native to Eastern Europe; introduced in **ballast** water; first discovered in 1990 near Detroit; in all Great Lakes by 1995

SPREAD BY: bait bucket transfers; high reproductive capacity; can spawn up to 6 times per summer

HOW YOU CAN HELP:

Gobies will often try to steal bait from anglers fishing near the bottom for perch or walleye. As a consequence, anglers are often the first to encounter gobies in a new habitat. Do not use them as bait!

- **CLEAN • DRAIN • DRY** page 20
- **REPORT** new inland sightings to your state's natural resource agency (page 124); note date, exact location (page 128) and include a photograph, if possible
- Freeze specimen (or preserve in rubbing alcohol) and report

One of the more annoying ways they impact anglers is by stealing bait from hooks!

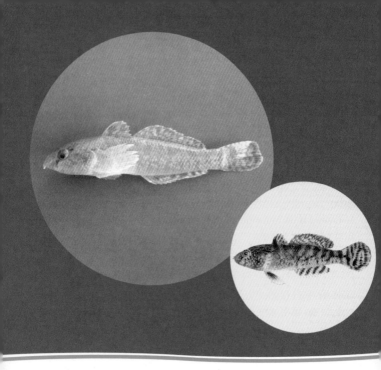

IMPACT ON YOU!

Tubenose gobies compete with, and prey upon, native bottom-dwelling fish. Their preferred habitat impacts the spawning grounds and nurseries of native fish species.

- Eats fish larvae and fish eggs
- Competes with native fish for food, feeding on invertebrates, insect nymphs and small **crustaceans**

For more information go to www.usgs.gov or scan this code with your smart phone. See page 31 for details.

Tubenose goby

Proterorhinus semilunaris

OTHER COMMON NAMES: goby

DESCRIPTION: up to 4 inches; mottled brown body, usually 5 dark bars on sides; a single scallop-shaped **pelvic fin** (resembles a suction cup); nostrils extend beyond lower **lip** and are tube-like; black lines on first **dorsal fin**

COMPARE: sculpin and other native species have a pair of pelvic fins; the round goby (page 101) is the only other invasive with a single fused pelvic fin

HABITAT: inshore bottom areas with plant cover in lakes and rivers; defends its nest sites created under rocks, logs and shells

ORIGIN: native to Eastern Europe; introduced to the Great Lakes in **ballast** water; first detected in the St. Clair River in 1990; not dispersed as widely as the round goby (page 101)

SPREAD BY: use of live bait and potentially bait bucket transfer; further ballast releases

HOW YOU CAN HELP:

Tubenose gobies lay eggs on vegetation, so it's important to remove all plant material from boats and trailers. Don't use gobies as bait and do not release alive!

- **CLEAN • DRAIN • DRY** page 20
- **REPORT** a catch or new sighting to your state's natural resource agency (page 124); note date, exact location (page 128) and include a photograph, if possible
- Freeze specimen (or preserve in rubbing alcohol) and report

Their suction cup-like fin allows them to hang onto objects on the bottom in flowing water.

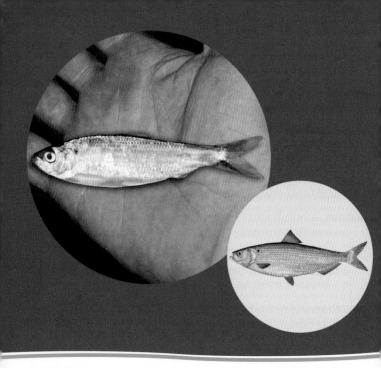

IMPACT ON YOU!

The introduction of blueback herring into lakes has coincided with a decrease in game fish, such as largemouth bass and walleye.

- Preys on eggs and larvae of native fish
- Feeds heavily on **zooplankton**, the food for young native fish

For more information go to www.usgs.gov or scan this code with your smart phone. See page 31 for details.

Blueback herring
Alosa aestivalis

OTHER COMMON NAMES: river herring, blueback shad, blueback, glut herring, big-eye

DESCRIPTION: 5–12 inches; silvery, deep bluish-green back; **scutes** along belly; lower jaw rises steeply, no teeth

COMPARE: dissection is required to differentiate it from alewife (page 91); the lining of the alewife body cavity is white, while the blueback herring's is purple

HABITAT: deep, open waters; spawns spring to early summer in rivers and streams

ORIGIN: native to Atlantic Coast; stocked as food for game fish in southern reservoirs; discovered in Lake Ontario in 1995 (entering via the **New York State Canal System**); likely to find suitable habitat throughout the Great Lakes, except possibly the deeper waters of Lake Superior

SPREAD BY: release of live bait; range expansion along interconnected waterways

 HOW YOU CAN HELP:

If blueback herring become established in Lake Ontario, they could spread to other Great Lakes, slowing recovery of native fishes, such as lake trout and cisco. Don't use them for bait!

- **CLEAN • DRAIN • DRY** page 20
- **REPORT** new inland sightings to your state's natural resource agency (page 124); note date, exact location (page 128) and include a photograph, if possible
- Freeze specimen (or preserve in rubbing alcohol) and report

On the East Coast, blueback herring and alewives are often called "river herring."

IMPACT ON YOU!

Anglers who fish for lake trout, salmon, steelhead, brown trout, whitefish, yellow perch, burbot, walleye and catfish are affected by this parasitic invader; each lamprey kills an estimated 40 pounds of fish in its lifetime.

- One of the most devastating aquatic invasive species in the Great Lakes
- Contributed to the **extirpation** of lake trout in all of the Great Lakes, except Lake Superior

For more information go to www.usgs.gov or scan this code with your smart phone. See page 31 for details.

Sea lamprey
Petromyzon marinus

OTHER COMMON NAMES: green lamprey, lamper, lake lamprey, eel sucker, lamprey eel, nine eyes, shad lamprey, spotted lamprey

DESCRIPTION: 12–20 inches; jawless, parasitic, eel-like fish; gray-blue back, metallic violet sides, silver-white belly; suction-cup mouth, hook-like teeth, rasping tongue

COMPARE: native freshwater lamprey species are smaller and mostly found in rivers and streams; they live in balance with the **food chain** and don't deplete fish populations

HABITAT: adults spawn in streams and die in spring; larvae burrow into the stream bottoms, feeding on debris and **algae** for 3–17 years, then transform into parasitic adults; they then migrate back into the lake for 12–20 months, feeding on fish

ORIGIN: native to North Atlantic Ocean; entered Lake Erie via the **Welland Canal** in 1921; spread to all Great Lakes by 1938

SPREAD BY: one adult lays more than 100,000 eggs; despite a 90 percent population reduction in most areas, sea lampreys remain a threat

HOW YOU CAN HELP:

Sea lampreys caused disastrous declines in Great Lakes trout and whitefish in the 1940–50s, resulting in hundreds of millions of dollars in damage to commercial/sport fisheries. Since 1956, the United States and Canada have led a successful control program, but it costs more than $18 million annually.

- Support legislation that maintains the sea lamprey control program
- If you catch fish with lamprey attached, kill the lamprey

Sea lampreys bore into fish to feed on their blood and body fluids; under some conditions, only 1 out of 7 victims survives.

IMPACT ON YOU!

White perch feed heavily on the eggs and young of important game species, and they have the potential to cause declines in native fish populations.

- Competes with native fish for food and habitat
- Can **hybridize** with native white bass
- By 1952, it became the most numerous fish in Lake Erie

For more information go to www.usgs.gov or scan this code with your smart phone. See page 31 for details.

White perch
Morone americana

OTHER COMMON NAMES: narrow-mouthed bass, silver perch, perch, bass, sea perch, gray perch, blue nose perch, humpy

DESCRIPTION: 5–7 inches (can reach 15); grayish green to dark green-brown, silver sides, silvery white belly

COMPARE: similar body shape to white bass (*Morone chrysops*) but deepest just ahead of the **dorsal fin**; no dark lines on back or sides; when the spiny dorsal fin is pulled erect, the soft dorsal fin rises also; the 2nd and 3rd anal spines are equal lengths; no spots between rays like the ruffe; the 3 bony **anal fin** spines on the white bass are different lengths and arranged in ascending order

HABITAT: **brackish** water, adapted to freshwater; river mouths, bays, reefs, nearshore areas; spawns in tributaries along the Great Lakes in April and May

ORIGIN: native to Atlantic Coast; entered lower Great Lakes in early 1950s through the Hudson River–Erie barge canal system and spread westward

SPREAD BY: accidental inclusion in shipments for stocking inland lakes

 HOW YOU CAN HELP:

White perch is a "prohibited invasive species" in several states.

- **CLEAN • DRAIN • DRY** page 20
- **REPORT** a catch or new inland sightings to your state's natural resource agency (page 124); note date, exact location (page 128) and include a photograph, if possible
- Freeze specimen (or preserve in rubbing alcohol) and report

Low-value, non-native white perch now dominate commercial fishing net catches in Lake Erie.

IMPACT ON YOU!

Rudd can **hybridize** with golden shiners; this can cause genetic problems in wild shiner populations.

- Feeds heavily on aquatic plants, releasing nutrients that lower water quality
- Puts vulnerable native plant communities at risk
- In areas with rudd populations, native fish spawning is less successful

For more information go to www.usgs.gov or scan this code with your smart phone. See page 31 for details.

Rudd
Scardinius erythrophthalmus

OTHER COMMON NAMES: rudd, redeye, pearl roach

DESCRIPTION: up to 19 inches; golden bronze body, white belly; bright red-orange **fins**; protruding lower jaw; iris of eye has a red spot above the pupil

COMPARE: has a scaled **keel** along belly, from **pelvic** to **anal fins**; the native golden shiner (*Notemigonus crysoleucas*) has no scales on keel

HABITAT: still, surface waters of shallow weedy shorelines in lakes, river backwaters, canals; seldom moves to open water

ORIGIN: native to Europe and Central Asia; brought to the United States in early 1900s as a food and game species; Arkansas fish farmers began culturing for bait industry in early 1980s

SPREAD BY: accidently mixed into shiner shipments to bait dealers; unintentionally released into new waters by anglers; range expansion via connected waterways

 HOW YOU CAN HELP:

Learn how to identify rudd. As you bait your hook, take a look. Rudd is illegal to use as bait in many states, so know your regulations. If it is different from the others, dispose in trash.

- **CLEAN • DRAIN • DRY** page 20
- **REPORT** a catch or new sighting to your state's natural resource agency (page 124); note date, exact location (page 128) and include a photograph, if possible
- Freeze specimen (or preserve in rubbing alcohol) and report

Unlike most native fish, rudd can switch diets, going from insects and minnows to aquatic plants.

IMPACT ON YOU!

Eurasian ruffe have a diverse diet, live in a variety of habitats, and reproduce and grow rapidly, allowing them to be a successful invader.

- Competes with and displaces native species in newly invaded areas
- Native predators eat them but not enough to keep their populations in check

For more information go to www.usgs.gov or scan this code with your smart phone. See page 31 for details.

Eurasian ruffe
Gymnocephalus cernuus

OTHER COMMON NAMES: ruffe, river ruffe, pope, porcupine fish

DESCRIPTION: up to 10 inches; olive to golden-brown with a whitish belly; spiny and soft **dorsal fins** connected; rows of dark spots in between spines; face exhibits a permanent "frown"; slimy and spiny when handled

COMPARE: can be confused with young sauger (which also have spots between dorsal fin rays) but are quite spiny and slimy

HABITAT: lakes, large and small rivers, estuaries, ponds; from 1 to 250 feet deep; dark waters

ORIGIN: native to Central and Eastern Europe; introduced into Duluth harbor around 1985 via **ballast** water; spread to rivers and bays along the south shore of western Lake Superior and coastal habitats in Lakes Michigan and Huron

SPREAD BY: continuing inter-lake ballast releases; range expansion

👉 **HOW YOU CAN HELP:**

Eurasian ruffe are capable of explosive population growth and dominate fisheries. Do not use them as live bait!

- **CLEAN • DRAIN • DRY** page 20
- **REPORT** new sightings to your state's natural resource agency (page 124); note date, exact location (page 128) and include a photograph, if possible
- Freeze specimen (or preserve in rubbing alcohol) and report

Can feed in total darkness, a competitive advantage over many native fish.

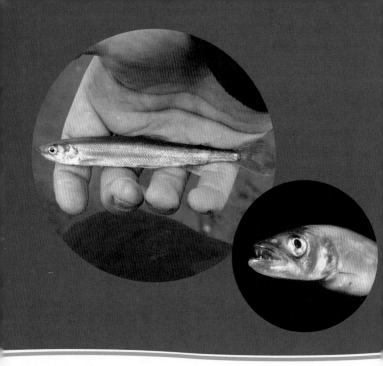

IMPACT ON YOU!

Evidence shows that after rainbow smelt move into a lake, they can decimate walleye populations. They are also known to negatively impact other native game fish.

- Eats the young of lake trout, cisco, whitefish, walleye . . . and their own!
- Implicated in the decline of native Great Lakes fish due to predation and **early life mortality syndrome**

For more information go to www.usgs.gov or scan this code with your smart phone. See page 31 for details.

Rainbow smelt

Osmerus mordax

OTHER COMMON NAMES: smelt, freshwater smelt, American smelt

DESCRIPTION: up to 12 inches; shimmers colorfully in water but out of water fades quickly and smells like cucumbers; has an adipose fin; large teeth on jaws and tongue; large mouth, protruding lower jaw, upper jaw extends to middle of eye or beyond

HABITAT: landlocked in clear, cool, deep lakes; spawns in early spring along shorelines, rivers, streams; often schools in open water in summer

ORIGIN: native to Atlantic Coast and Lake Champlain; introduced into Crystal Lake, Michigan, as prey species in 1912; escaped and invaded the Great Lakes

SPREAD BY: use and release of live bait; illegal stocking

HOW YOU CAN HELP:

Its spread to inland lakes may be partly the result of anglers putting live smelt into bait buckets, where eggs and milt can mix, then unintentionally introducing them by dumping the mix into the water. Such disposal is illegal.

- **CLEAN • DRAIN • DRY** (page 20)
- **REPORT** new sightings to your state's natural resource agency (page 124); note date, exact location (page 128) and include a photograph, if possible
- Freeze specimen (or preserve in rubbing alcohol) and report
- States have differing laws regarding smelt (dead or alive)

Spawns in both streams and deep waters of the Great Lakes.

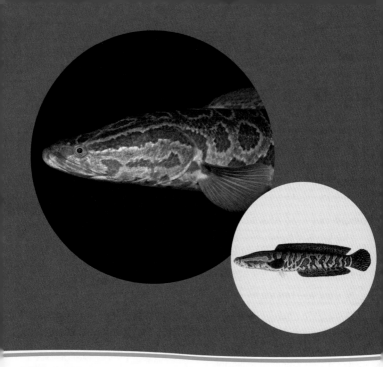

IMPACT ON YOU!

The northern snakehead is a voracious top-level predator with few natural enemies that reduces populations of native fish.

- Survives in water with very low oxygen, an advantage over trout, pike and bass
- Adapted to a wide range of environmental conditions
- Once established, very difficult to eradicate

For more information go to www.usgs.gov or scan this code with your smart phone. See page 31 for details.

Northern snakehead
Channa argus

OTHER COMMON NAMES: snakehead

DESCRIPTION: cylindrical body (up to 47 inches) is dark brown to tan with irregular blotches; long single **dorsal fin** and long **anal fin**; large scales on head give a "snakehead" appearance; jaws have canine-like teeth

COMPARE: the native bowfin (*Amia calva*) has a short anal fin and no scales on its head; native burbot (*Lota lota*) has 2 dorsal fins, a single **barbel** on the middle of chin and very tiny scales

HABITAT: muddy or vegetated ponds, swamps, slow-moving streams

ORIGIN: native to China; introduced by consumers after purchase from live-food markets or as released pets; first discovered in Crofton, Maryland, in 2002

SPREAD BY: aquarium releases; live-food release

HOW YOU CAN HELP:

All species of snakeheads have recently been given "injurious wildlife" status. If you think you've caught a snakehead—**do not release it alive!**

- **REPORT** your catch or a sighting to your state's natural resource agency (page 124)
- Note date, exact location (page 128) and photograph, if possible
- Freeze specimen (or preserve in rubbing alcohol) and report

Can breathe air, survive for three days out of water and can crawl overland.

IMPACT ON YOU!

A breeding threespine stickleback may look like a punk rocker, but it's an aggressive invader preying on native species and competing for food and habitat.

- Eats eggs and larvae of native fish
- May **hybridize** with native sticklebacks
- Stout spines discourage predators

For more information go to www.usgs.gov or scan this code with your smart phone. See page 31 for details.

Threespine stickleback
Gasterosteus aculeatus

OTHER COMMON NAMES: twospine stickleback, banstickle, spanstickle, saw-finned stickleback, eastern stickleback, tittlebat

DESCRIPTION: up to 4 inches; silvery with dark mottling; 3 stout dorsal spines (first two are longer than the third); large eyes; body scaleless with bony plates; breeding fish are colorful and defend their nests aggressively; nests on aquatic vegetation

COMPARE: native brook stickleback *(Culaea inconstans)* has 5–6 short dorsal spines; ninespine stickleback *(Pungitius pungitius)* has 9 short dorsal spines

HABITAT: can live in both salt water and fresh water; shores of larger lakes; shallow, sandy weedy areas in rivers, streams, ponds

ORIGIN: native off both coasts of the United States and Lake Ontario; in early 1980s spread to Lake Michigan, most likely from **ballast** water, canals and bait bucket transfers; now established in other Great Lakes

SPREAD BY: range expansion via canals and diversions; ballast water

👉 HOW YOU CAN HELP:

The most effective way to control any aquatic invasive species is to prevent new introductions and the spread of existing populations.

- **CLEAN • DRAIN • DRY** (page 20)
- **REPORT** new sightings to your state's natural resource agency (page 124); note date, exact location (page 128) and include a photograph, if possible
- Freeze specimen (or preserve in rubbing alcohol) and report

Anglers report sticklebacks are so aggressive they will attack a penny dropped into the water.

IMPACT ON YOU!

When redear sunfish are introduced, it can result in a reduction of as much as 56 percent of the native pumpkinseed population and 69 percent of native snails.

- Competes with adult pumpkinseeds for snails (both species' main adult food)
- Can alter the diet of the pumpkinseed sunfish, reducing its growth and abundance

For more information go to www.usgs.gov or scan this code with your smart phone. See page 31 for details.

Redear sunfish
Lepomis microlophus

OTHER COMMON NAMES: shellcracker, stumpknocker, cherry gill, sun perch, Georgia bream, chinquapin, rouge ear

DESCRIPTION: 8–9½ inches; hind end of **gill** flap is black with a white border and a red spot on tip (hence its name); pan-shaped, like other sunfish; olive with darker spots and flecks of red; chest is yellowish to cream; small mouth (barely reaches eye)

HABITAT: ponds, marshes, lakes; mud or sand bottom; sluggish to slow-moving water in streams and rivers; waters rich in vegetation and snags

ORIGIN: native to the southeast and the Mississippi River Basin to Indiana and Illinois

SPREAD BY: intentional stocking; aquarium releases; potential movement by anglers from stocked ponds

HOW YOU CAN HELP:

Never transport any live fish unless you have a stocking permit.

- **CLEAN • DRAIN • DRY** (page 20)
- **REPORT** new sightings to your state's natural resource agency (page 124); note date, exact location (page 128) and include a photograph, if possible
- Freeze specimen (or preserve in rubbing alcohol) and report

*Special **pharyngeal teeth** in their throat are used to crush a snail's shell, earning them the name "shellcracker."*

121

IMPACT ON YOU!

The tench has a tendency to stir up the muddy bottom where it lives.
The fine sediments can suffocate eggs and newly hatched fish of
native species, such as pike, perch or crappie.

- A potential competitor for food with trout and other game fish
- Consumes a wide variety of native bottom-dwelling organisms
- Can spawn in batches from spring to fall

For more information go to www.usgs.gov or scan this code
with your smart phone. See page 31 for details.

Tench
Tinca tinca

OTHER COMMON NAMES: doctor fish

DESCRIPTION: up to 18 inches; slimy, stocky carp-like shape; olive-green, darker above and almost golden below; small, red-orange eyes; small **barbel** at each corner of mouth; **fins** dark and rounded

HABITAT: muddy bottoms of lakes and slow-moving waterways; dense aquatic plant growth; dormant in winter, stays in the mud without feeding

ORIGIN: native of Eurasia; imported from Germany in 1877; beginning in 1880s was lawfully introduced for food and as a popular sport fish across the United States; escaped from holding facilities; released from **aquaculture** in late 1900s; intentional/illegal release in Lake Champlain; well established in the Mississippi River watershed and Lake Champlain

SPREAD BY: continued stocking for recreational angling; high reproductive rate

 HOW YOU CAN HELP:

Introduced as a popular sport fish in 38 states, tench are now considered an invasive species. They can outcompete native fish for food and habitat, disrupt the **food chain** and cause a general decline in water quality. Do not release them alive!

- **CLEAN • DRAIN • DRY** page 20
- **REPORT** new sightings to your state's natural resource agency (page 124); note date, exact location (page 128) and include a photograph, if possible
- Freeze specimen (or preserve in rubbing alcohol) and report

Survives in poorly oxygenated waters where even carp can't live.

STATE/FEDERAL/SEA GRANT OFFICES

Illinois
Illinois-Indiana Sea Grant College Program, University of Illinois
(217) 333-6444
www.iiseagrant.org

Illinois Department of Natural Resources, Springfield Office
(217) 782-6302
www.dnr.illinois.gov

Indiana
Illinois-Indiana Sea Grant College Program, University of Illinois
(217) 333-6444
www.iiseagrant.org

Indiana Department of Natural Resources, Indianapolis Office
(317) 232-4200
www.in.gov/dnr

Michigan
Michigan Sea Grant
(734) 763-1437
www.miseagrant.umich.edu

Michigan Department of Natural Resources Executive Office
(517) 373-2329
www.michigan.gov/dnr

Minnesota
Minnesota Sea Grant
(218) 726-8106
www.seagrant.umn.edu

Minnesota Department of Natural Resources
(651) 296-6157
www.dnr.state.mn.us

Resources Invasive Species Specialists
1-888-MINNDNR or (651) 259-5100
www.mndnr.gov/invasives/contacts.html

New York
New York Sea Grant
(631) 632-6905
www.seagrant.sunysb.edu

New York State Department of Environmental Conservation
(518) 402-8545
www.dec.ny.gov/

Ohio
Ohio Sea Grant College Program
(614) 292-8949
ohioseagrant.osu.edu

Ohio Department of Natural Resources Administrative Office
(614) 265-6565
www.ohiodnr.com

Pennsylvania
Pennsylvania Sea Grant
(814) 217-9012
www.seagrant.psu.edu

Pennsylvania Fish and Boat Commission
(717) 705-7800
www.fish.state.pa.us

Vermont
Lake Champlain Sea Grant
(802) 656-0682
www.uvm.edu/seagrant

Vermont Agency of Natural Resources
(802) 241-3600
www.anr.state.vt.us/

Wisconsin
University of Wisconsin Sea Grant Institute
(920) 683-4697
www.seagrant.wisc.edu

Wisconsin Department of Natural Resources, Central Office
(608) 266-2621
dnr.wi.gov

UNITED STATES FOREST SERVICE
www.fs.fed.us/r9/wildlife/nnis

Eastern Regional Office-R9
626 East Wisconsin Avenue
Milwaukee, WI 53202
(414) 297-3600
Fax: (414) 297-3808

UNITED STATES FISH AND WILDLIFE SERVICE
www.ProtectYourWaters.net

Midwest Regional Office (IL, IN, MI, MN, OH, WI)
5600 American Boulevard West
Bloomington, MN 55437-1458
(612) 713-5360

Northeast Regional Office (NY, PA, VT)
300 Westgate Center Drive
Hadley, MA 01035-9587
(413) 253-8200

NATIONAL PARK SERVICE
Great Lakes Early Detection Network
University of Wisconsin-Madison
Madison, WI 53706
www.GLEDN.org

Midwest Regional Office (IL, IN, MI, MN, OH, WI)
601 Riverfront Drive
Omaha, NE 68102-4226
(402) 661-1736

Northeast Regional Office (NY, PA, VT)
U.S. Custom House
200 Chestnut Street, Fifth Floor
Philadelphia, PA 19106
(215) 597-7013

NOAA GREAT LAKES ENVIRONMENTAL RESEARCH LABORATORY

4840 South State Road
Ann Arbor, MI 48108-9719
(734) 741-2287
www.glerl.noaa.gov

GREAT LAKES INDIAN FISH AND WILDLIFE COMMISSION

PO Box 9
72682 Maple Street
Odanah, WI 54861
(715) 682-6619
www.glifwc.org

ONTARIO FEDERATION OF ANGLERS AND HUNTERS

PO Box 2800
4601 Guthrie Drive
Peterborough, Ontario, K9J 8L5
(705) 748-6324 ext. 274
www.ofah.org

TEMPLATE FOR NOTING SIGHTING DETAILS

WHAT? Description and General Group—e.g., fish, plant, parasite
(species, if you know it)

_____

_____

_____

WHEN? Date _____ Time _____

WHERE?
GPS Coordinates (if available)_____

Location (state, county, site) _____

PHOTOGRAPH(S) TAKEN? _____

_____

_____

SPECIMEN? _____

_____

_____

COMMENTS: _____

_____

_____

NOTE: GLANSIS (Great Lakes Aquatic Nonindigenous Species
Information System) uses the reporting interface at the URL below.
It works from anywhere in the United States Report a sighting!
http://nas.er.usgs.gov/SightingReport.aspx

TEMPLATE FOR NOTING SIGHTING DETAILS

WHAT? Description and General Group—e.g., fish, plant, parasite (species, if you know it)

_____

_____

_____

WHEN? Date _____ Time _____

WHERE?
GPS Coordinates (if available)_____

Location (state, county, site) _____

PHOTOGRAPH(S) TAKEN? _____

_____

_____

SPECIMEN? _____

_____

_____

COMMENTS: _____

_____

_____

NOTE: GLANSIS (Great Lakes Aquatic Nonindigenous Species Information System) uses the reporting interface at the URL below. It works from anywhere in the United States Report a sighting! http://nas.er.usgs.gov/SightingReport.aspx

ABOUT THE NATIONAL PROFESSIONAL ANGLERS ASSOCIATION

The National Professional Anglers Association (NPAA), founded in 1997, is a non-profit association comprised of anglers who are committed to giving back to the sport they love. The NPAA has two main goals:

1. Grow the sport of fishing

2. Increase the professionalism of our members

Membership consists of anglers who live to fish and are willing to share their passion for the sport with others. Many compete in tournament events, a large number are professional guides or charter captains and many work with fishing/marine industry companies to promote the sport of fishing. Each member has the ability to receive financial support from the NPAA for "Future Angler Events" they participate in or host, giving members an opportunity to give back to the sport they love by exposing potential future anglers of all ages to the sport.

Fortunately, NPAA members are well positioned to educate their fellow and future anglers about the risks of aquatic invasive species and the steps to avoid their spread.

To find out more about the NPAA, go to their website at www.NPAA.net.

ABOUT THE U.S. FOREST SERVICE

The mission of the U.S. Forest Service is to sustain the health, diversity and productivity of the nation's natural resources. The Eastern Region of the U.S. Forest Service, which encompasses the United States portion of the Great Lakes region, is rich in water.

National Forests in the region have more than 962,000 acres of lakes, 2 million acres of wetlands and 15,000 miles of streams.

These ecosystems provide clean drinking water for communities, healthy habitat for fish and wildlife, and recreational opportunities for millions of visitors.

Invasive species threaten these tremendous resources. The U.S. Forest Service seeks to reduce, minimize or eliminate the potential for introduction, establishment, spread and impact of terrestrial and aquatic invasive species across all landscapes and ownerships. Partnerships are critical in our mission to sustain world-class natural resources and diverse recreation for the use and enjoyment of all.

Visit www.fs.fed.us/r9 and www.fs.fed.us/invasivespecies to learn more.

Website for public users: www.fs.fed.us/r9/wildlife/nnis

Phone contact: John Rothlisberger, Aquatic Ecologist, U.S. Forest Service, Eastern Region, (414)297-1749

ABOUT THE U.S. FISH AND WILDLIFE SERVICE

The U.S. Fish and Wildlife Service (Service) is the only agency of the U.S. Government whose primary responsibility is the conservation of our nation's fish, wildlife and plants. Invasive species degrade habitats and compete with native animals and plants.

The Service works to prevent the introduction of invasive species in the Great Lakes and elsewhere in United States, and to contain, control and eradicate species that invade our ecosystems. Detecting invasive species before populations become established, and documenting distribution and abundance of established populations are important elements in a comprehensive approach to Great Lakes invasive species management.

This guide will help better detect and identify invasive species in and around the Great Lakes, and provide tips on how to prevent further invasive spread. Communicating detections are vital for resource managers so they can take appropriate actions. The Service greatly appreciates the efforts of all involved in developing this guide.

ABOUT THE NATIONAL PARK SERVICE

 The National Park Service supports 11 national parks within the Great Lakes Basin. Working to preserve natural and cultural resources for the enjoyment, education and inspiration of this and future generations, the park service cooperates with many partners, extending benefits of conservation and outdoor recreation.

The National Park Service is one of America's leading natural resource agencies and a leader in fighting invasive species.

For more information on how you can help stop invasive species and report new sightings, visit the Great Lakes Early Detection Network (GLEDN) online. Here you will find a valuable resource to share information on the location of invasive species.

If you find invasive species on parklands or any other location, please report them at www.GLEDN.org.

ABOUT THE STATE-FISH ART™ PROGRAM

Wildlife Forever teaches aquatic conservation to America's youth through the ART OF CONSERVATION's State-Fish Art Program, using art as a springboard into the fascinating world of fish.

"Fish On!," the CD-ROM Lesson Plan, brings aquatic education into K-12 classrooms nationwide and includes extension tools on aquatic invasive species identification and awareness. The invasive lesson, "Making Waves," was developed by Wildlife Forever's international partner, the Ontario Federation of Hunters and Anglers. It takes youth through fun activities while learning about invasive species, fish, and fisheries conservation.

The State-Fish Art Program culminates in a national contest where kids submit art and an essay about their chosen state fish. A special "Silent Invader" entry category requires the artwork and essay include both a designated fish and invasive species. The national winner is recognized with the year's "Invader Crusader" award.

The program is available at no charge and is successfully advancing invasive species education by creating a new generation of stewards who understand the threats. For more information, visit www.statefishart.org.

ABOUT THE THREAT CAMPAIGN™

 Invasive Species are one of the greatest conservation challenges facing our natural resources. They destroy habitat and are one of the leading causes for fish and wildlife to be added to threatened and endangered species lists.

The Threat Campaign is an award-winning national partnership of state, federal, tribal and non-governmental organizations and ordinary citizens working together to educate the public on awareness and prevention of invasive species. Using numerous multimedia tools, the Threat Campaign includes public service announcements, grassroots education and outreach events to inform those who play and work outdoors.

CLEAN • DRAIN • DRY are the most important steps you can take to ensure healthy fish and wildlife. Learn more at: www.CleanDrainDry.org

Help stop invasive species from ruining your favorite fishing spot or outdoor location. Join Wildlife Forever today.

ABOUT THE STOP AQUATIC HITCHHIKERS! CAMPAIGN

A National Public Awareness and Partnership Campaign on Aquatic Invasive Species

STOP AQUATIC HITCHHIKERS!™

Stop Aquatic Hitchhikers! is a national public awareness campaign focused on education and prevention of aquatic invasive species. Designed by the U.S. Fish and Wildlife Service in partnership with many state, federal and various organizations, the multi-faceted campaign raises awareness with aquatic recreational users. Promoting environmentally friendly behaviors of **CLEAN • DRAIN • DRY**, consistent messaging and brand awareness reinforces prevention steps individuals can take to protect water resources from the damaging effects of invasive species.

Join the campaign!

Anyone can join the campaign and become an active prevention partner. By signing up, you will receive marketing tools and materials that will allow you to take the branded campaign message to your community. Help inform and educate others on aquatic invasive species prevention. Join Stop Aquatic Hitchhikers! today.

Visit www.CleanDrainDry.net to learn more.

WILDLIFE FOREVER

2700 Freeway Blvd., #1000
Brooklyn Center, MN 55430
(763) 253-0222
www.WildlifeForever.org

GLOSSARY

adaptation particular characteristic developed that makes it better suited to its environment

adipose fin a fin on many fish located behind the dorsal fin; often clipped on hatchery fish so that people can tell them from wild fish NOTE: not shown on the picture diagram (page 87)

algae plants that are usually aquatic, ranging in size from single cells to large seaweeds, and lack true stems, roots and leaves

algal bloom occurs in both marine and freshwater during suitable environmental conditions when algae responds to nutrients in the water and reproduces rapidly; some produce potent chemical toxins

amphibian cold-blooded, smooth-skinned vertebrates that spend part of their life on land and part of their life in the water, including frogs, toads, newts and salamanders

anadromous fish that spend most of their life in salt water but migrate to freshwater to spawn

angler person who catches fish or attempts to catch fish for food or recreation

annual plant that completes its life cycle in one year or less

anterior situated forward, toward the head end

aperture the hole at the base of a snail's shell through which the body comes out

aquaculture cultivation of freshwater and marine resources, both plant and animal, for human consumption or use

aquatic of, in or pertaining to water

aquatic insect insects that spend all or part of their lives in water (e.g., mayflies)

aquatic plant plant that grows partly or wholly in water, whether rooted in the mud or floating

axis the main stem or central part around which plant parts, such as branches, are arranged

bait natural, processed and artificial objects used to catch fish

ballast material (rocks or water) taken onboard ships to help maintain stability when the cargo hold is empty

barb sharp, spur-like projection

barbel slender, fleshy, flexible projection near the mouth of certain fish, including catfish and carp; used for smell and taste

basal pertaining to the base of a plant or stem

behavior way an organism responds to its environment

benthic relating or pertaining to the bottom or lowermost levels of a sea or lake

bilge the area in the bottom of a boat, usually near the stern, where water collects

biodiversity the variety of lifeforms within an ecosystem and a measure of its health

biofoul attachment of an organism or organisms to a surface in contact with water for a period of time; can eventually cause corrosion (e.g., hulls of ships, fishing equipment, water cooling systems)

biologist person who studies the science of living organisms and life processes

bivalve second-most diverse group of mollusks, easily recognized by its two-halved shell, including mussels, oysters and scallops

bottom-dwelling living on or in sea, lake or river bottoms

botulism poisoning by botulinum toxin, one of the most potent toxins known

brackish slightly salty or briny water

brood (verb) to hatch, protect and warm the young, usually done instinctively by the female

burrow (verb) to dig underground

byssal thread strong, silky fiber made from proteins that is used by mussels to attach to rocks, pilings or other surfaces

camouflage protective adaptation that enables an organism to disguise itself or blend with its surroundings

carapace the part of the shell covering the head and thorax of a crab or crayfish

carnivore eats only meat

catch-and-release practice of catching game fish using sporting methods and releasing them alive and unharmed; catch-and-release is used as a wildlife management tool designed to increase fish populations by restricting the number of fish caught and kept by anglers, as well as regulating the size and type of the fish caught

cluster (noun) number of things of the same kind, growing or held together; (verb) to gather into a cluster

clutch nest of eggs

colony group of organisms that prefers to live together

communication sound, scent or behavior recognized by members of the same species (see also "pheromone" and "courtship")

competition the struggle between different species that use the same source for food or shelter

conchologist person who studies mollusks and shells

conservation care, wise use and management of a resource

courtship behavior or series of actions a fish displays to indicate to the opposite sex that it is ready to mate in order to reproduce

cover naturally occurring sheltered areas that provide concealment and shelter for wildlife, such as a dead tree, fallen log, rock outcrops or dense areas of plants

crustacean group of mostly aquatic animals that have an exterior skeleton and antennae; some examples of crustaceans include shrimps, lobsters, crabs and water fleas

cylindrical long, roller-shaped body with circles at the two ends, with straight sides between

detritus the broken-down remains of dead plants and animals, and the bacteria living in or on it

diatom a unicellular organism and one of the most common types of phytoplankton; both abundant and of vital importance, thought to produce at least a quarter of our oxygen

die-off when a large number of organisms (plants or animals) die suddenly in a short timeframe; a common cause of summer fish kills occurs when a dense growth of submerged aquatic plants or algae dies suddenly from natural causes and decomposes, using up all the oxygen in the water; this leaves none for other aquatic organisms, such as fish

diurnal active during the day

dorsal upper surface of an organism; the top

early life mortality syndrome a thiamin deficiency in young fish, primarily lake trout, caused by a maternal diet high in smelt or alewife

ecology study of the relationships between living things and the environment in which they live

ecosystem interacting system of plants, animals, soil and climactic conditions in a self-contained environment (e.g., pond, marsh, swamp, lake or stream)

emergent aquatic plants which have some portion of the plant extended out of the water

endangered species in danger of becoming extinct due to declining population numbers

environment entire surroundings of an organism or group of organisms

eradicate completely eliminate from an area

Erie Canal a 363-mile-long waterway in New York that runs from the Atlantic Ocean to the Great Lakes; opened in 1825, now part of the New York State Canal System

estuary area where freshwater and salt water meet, and the area where rivers dump into lakes

ethics principles of good conduct; a sense of right and wrong

exotic an organism from another region or ecosystem that may be considered undesirable as it competes with native species for habitat and food (see "invasive species")

extinct species that no longer exists or has died out

extirpation to remove totally from an area

face a flat side

filter-feed feed by straining suspended matter and food particles from water, typically by passing the water over a specialized filtering structure

fin membranous appendage extending from the body of a fish or other aquatic animal, used for propelling, steering or balancing the body in the water (see page 87)

fin thread long, threadlike last ray of the dorsal fin

fishery biologist person who manages aquatic and wetland habitats and fish reproduction and health

fishing line cord used or made for angling

food chain plants and animals linked together as sources and consumers of food; typically an organism higher in the food chain eats the one lower in the food chain, so the health of one is dependent on the health of another

food web the many possible feeding relationships found within a given ecosystem

forage (noun) plant material; (verb) to eat plant material

foul make foul or dirty; pollute

fragment small plant piece broken off (often by boat propellers) or detached naturally

fragmentation one method by which an aquatic plant spreads; a single tiny fragment that contains at least one node is capable of rooting and growing into a new plant

freshwater body of water that contains little salt (e.g., pond, lake or stream)

fruit plant structure that bears the seeds

fry newly hatched young fish

game fish fish that can be caught according to legal seasons and limits

gill respiratory organ in mollusks, crustaceans and fish that obtains oxygen from the water and releases carbon dioxide

habitat local environment in which one lives; includes food, water, cover (shelter) and space

herbivore eats only plant material

hermaphroditic having reproductive organs of both sexes

hibernation period of winter dormancy during which body processes slow dramatically, reducing the amount of energy required for survival

home range area over which an animal repeatedly travels in order to locate food, water and cover

host animal or plant in or on which another organism lives

hybridize sexual reproduction between two different recognized species

ichthyology study of fish

immersed beneath the surface of the water

immune system body system made up of many organs and cells that defends against infection, disease and foreign substances

incubate the time for an embryo to develop in an egg prior to hatching

instinct inherited or unlearned behavior

invasive species plants, animals, fish or diseases brought from another region, often another continent, either intentionally or by accident, that have a negative effect on the native species as they compete for habitat and food (also referred to as exotic, non-native or introduced species)

invertebrates animals without backbones, including insects, earthworms, spiders and mollusks

keel sharp, longitudinal fold or ridge, usually on the ventral side of a fish

landlocked living in waters shut off from the sea, as in some fish

larva (singular) **larvae** (plural) newly hatched, earliest stage that differs greatly from the appearance and form of an adult

lateral line system of sensory nerves in the skin, extending from head to tail on either side of a fish, that detects movement of water and other fish

leaf blade-like organ attached to the stem, commonly functioning as a principal organ in photosynthesis

leaflet one of many leaf-like structures that make up a leaf

leafstalk (petiole) stem-like structure that attaches a leaf to the main stem

limiting factor environmental component, such as drought, extreme cold and shortage of food or cover, that negatively impacts wildlife and plant populations

lip wall of the opening made by the last complete turn of the shell in snails

littoral zone (freshwater) region close to shore. Sunlight reaches all the way to the bottom, allowing rooted aquatic plants to grow, creating a habitat for fish and other organisms that is very different from open water.

livewell compartment in a boat designed to hold water (typically recirculating) and keep fish alive

lure artificial object used to catch fish

macrofoul clogging of screens and other hard-surfaced components in raw water systems because of living organisms

margin edge or border of a leaf

marine aquatic habitat in salt water

migration seasonal movements of fish and wildlife from one area to another that are usually triggered by environmental cues, such as day length, temperature or water flow

milt semen of a male fish that fertilizes the female's eggs during spawning

Mississippi River Basin the fourth-largest watershed in the world covering much of the central United States; drained by the Mississippi River System from its origin in Minnesota, east to the Appalachian Mountains, west to the Rocky Mountains and emptying into the Gulf of Mexico in Louisiana

mollusk or **mollusc** invertebrates with smooth, soft bodies, including clams, snails, oysters, slugs, octopuses and squid

multiple-use using and managing an area to provide more than one benefit simultaneously

nacreous, **nacre** pertaining to the pearly lining of a mussel shell

native indigenous or naturally occurring species

natural resource material found in nature to which people have assigned value

New York State Canal System (NYSCS) a 524-mile canal system across New York State linking the Great Lakes with the Hudson River

nocturnal active at night

node point along a stem which gives rise to leaves, branches or flowers

nongame species the fish and wildlife not often sought for sport by humans

nonrenewable natural resource nonliving natural resources that, for all practical purposes, cannot be replaced, including metallic minerals and fossil fuels

noxious weed any plant designated by a federal, state or county government as injurious to public health, agriculture, recreation, wildlife or property

nut hard, one-seeded fruit, typically with an outer shell

omnivore eats both plants and meat

operculum (mollusks) covering or lid that closes the opening; (fish) the cover protecting the gills

parasite organism, plant or animal, feeding on another

parthenogenesis form of reproduction in which an unfertilized egg develops into a new individual

pathogen a germ (such as a bacterium or virus) that causes disease

pathway way that serves as a path for something to move or spread

pelvic of, relating to, or located in or near the pelvis

perennial plant that lives for more than two years

pharyngeal teeth teeth composed of hard, movable plates located in the throat of certain fish and used for crushing or grinding food

pheromone chemical scent secreted as a means of communication among members of the same species

photosynthesis process by which plant cells convert light, water and carbon dioxide into energy and nutrients while simultaneously releasing oxygen

phytoplankton plants and plantlike organisms in plankton; the very foundation of the aquatic food web; they are also responsible for consuming carbon dioxide from the atmosphere and releasing oxygen into the water

plankton group of passively floating or drifting organisms occurring in a body of water, primarily microscopic algae and protozoa; it is important as the base food source and all aquatic life is dependent upon the energy and oxygen it provides

pollution toxic (poisonous) substances deposited in the air, water or soil, creating an unhealthy environment

population collection of individuals of the same species in a given area whose members can breed with one another

posterior the rear; at the tail end

predator one that hunts and feeds on others (prey)

prey one that is hunted or killed for food by others (predators)

range particular geographic region in which a species is found

ray flexible support for a fin

recreation activity undertaken for enjoyment; entertainment often associated with natural resources, such as fishing, boating, bird watching, hiking and hunting

redd nest-like depression made by a male or female fish to contain eggs

renewable natural resource natural resource that can be replenished and harvested, including trees and wildlife

resting egg egg that has entered a phase of slowed or stopped development, sometimes over winter

rhizome stem that grows horizontally at or just below the soil surface, producing roots below and sending up shoots above

riparian area lands adjacent to streams, rivers, lakes and other wetlands where the vegetation is influenced by the great availability of water

riprap rock or other material used to protect shorelines, streambeds, bridge abutments, pilings and other shoreline structures against water or ice erosion

rosette dense cluster of leaves that are all at a single height, such as petals of a rose

salt water body of water with a high concentration of salt

scales small, flat plates that fit together to form the external body covering of a fish

school group of fish

scute modified, thickened scale that often is keeled or spiny

season pertaining to the window of time in which females are reproductively active to produce offspring

serrated (plant) leaf with sharp, typically forward-pointing, teeth

sinker small metal weight used by anglers designed to sink bait or lures

spawn process of fish reproduction; involves females laying eggs and males fertilizing them to produce young fish

species group that has a similar structure, common ancestors and characteristics that are maintained through breeding

sport fish certain species of fish that are actively pursued by anglers because they are considered challenging and/or fun to catch or they are desirable to eat (also called game fish)

stem principal shoot of a plant

stewardship responsible care of natural resources for future generations

stocking adding fish (usually game fish) to a body of water, such as a lake, pond or stream

stolon flat-lying or creeping plant structure that lies along the top of the ground, from which erect branches grow (a runner is a type of stolon)

stress factor that may negatively affect health, such as lack of food and/or habitat, disease or overpopulation

substrate surface or material on or from which an organism lives, grows or obtains its nourishment

suture spiral line marking the junction between whorls in mollusks

tackle fishing equipment (e.g., rods, reels, poles, lines, sinkers, hooks, bobbers and lures)

territory area defended, usually during breeding season, typically against members of its own species

threatened classification for species whose population is in great decline and approaching the endangered classification

tooth (plant) points or lobes along a leaf edge

toxic poisonous

transfer movement of live bait and water from one body of water to another

trematode parasitic flatworms having external suckers for attaching to a host

trolling to fish in by trailing a baited line or lines behind a boat

tuber potato-like or pealike swellings forming at the end of roots or on rhizomes that overwinter and sprout into new plants in the spring

turion hardy plant bud found on the stem of certain aquatic plants that detach, fall or drift on currents to the bottom, overwinter and grow into a new plant the following spring

valve half the shell of a bivalve

vector spreads infection by transporting pathogens from one host or place to another, but does not itself cause disease

veliger microscopic, free-swimming larva of some mollusks, such as zebra and quagga mussels

ventral lower surface of an organism; the bottom

vertebrate having a backbone, including fish, birds, mammals, reptiles and amphibians

viable (plant) able to begin to grow and put out shoots after a period of dormancy

Welland Canal built to go around Niagara Falls and connect Lake Ontario to Lake Erie, providing a man-made deep waterway to access the Great Lakes; the first Welland Canal opened in 1829; the present canal officially opened in 1932

whorl (plant) three or more leaves, forming a ringlike arrangement around the stem; (invertebrate) one turn of a spiral shell

wildlife non-domesticated animals (including mammals, birds, fish, reptiles, amphibians and insects)

wildlife agency state or federal organization responsible for managing wildlife

wildlife management combination of techniques, scientific knowledge and technical skills used to protect, conserve and manage wildlife and habitat

winterkill death during winter resulting from lack of oxygen due to deep snow cover and low oxygen production

zooplankton the animal constituent of plankton; mainly small crustaceans and fish larvae; populations of zooplankton feed on phytoplankton, and then, in turn, they provide nourishment for fish and crustaceans

KIDS LOVE TO LEARN ABOUT INVASIVE SPECIES!

Aquatic invasive species are like uninvited visitors from far away that come to your house, invite themselves in, eat your food and use your things . . . and they don't share. They take the food that you depend on. They crowd your living space and chase you out of your favorite spots.

In fact, they really, really, really like living in your home. It has everything they need! Their enemies are far away, so there isn't anyone around to get them under control. Once the visitors move in, they grow and multiply, and you can't get rid of them.

Pretty soon your home is not the healthy, special place it was before they showed up, and it gets harder and harder for you to live there. If only you had known how to prevent the invaders from coming in the first place!

Aquatic invasive species are like pollution: they are easiest to control by preventing the problem in the first place. Once something is polluted, it is difficult to manage, as the pollution is almost impossible to get rid of. Attempting to do so costs a lot of money now (and into the future). The same goes for aquatic invasive species. By learning about them and how they spread, we can prevent them from invading and finding new homes in our rivers, lakes and streams.

Aquatic invasive species most commonly spread on boats, trailers, fishing gear and recreational equipment. Fortunately, there are three steps you can take every time you leave any body of water to prevent invaders from hitching a ride to a new home. Learn about these steps on page 20.

Here is a list of websites just full of fun projects and activities you can do on your own or in your classroom, so share this information with your parents and teachers. Everyone can help stop the invasion and become an "Invader Crusader" to stop aquatic hitchhikers!

Nab the Aquatic Invader—Be a Sea Grant Super Sleuth
Check out many of the unusual species that create real problems in the Great Lakes:
www.iiseagrant.org/NabInvader/great_lakes.html

The Great Lakes Invasion
While creatures from another planet may not be real or a threat, creatures that threaten the Great Lakes do exist.
www.iisgcp.org/catalog/downlds_09/invasion.pdf

Be Part of the Search for Invasive Species
A step-by-step approach to seeing if you've found an invasive species.
www.glerl.noaa.gov/res/Programs/glansis/kids.html

EEK!—Alien Invaders
Read these stories and find out how to pick aliens out of a crowd:
http://dnr.wi.gov/org/caer/ce/eek/earth/aliens.htm

Habitattitude
Adopt a conservation mentality: protect our environment by not releasing unwanted fish and aquatic plants into the wild.
www.habitattitude.net/

Making Waves & State-Fish Art Contest
A fun, informative and activity-filled teacher resource kit that introduces children to the concept of healthy habitats and communities and our role in protecting them from aquatic invasive species. Then enter the State-Fish Art Contest (page 133).
www.wildlifeforever.org/contest/new2012/invasive_award
www.statefishart.org

Attack Packs
Rucksacks filled with materials help teach students and other groups about Great Lakes aquatic invasive species, the problems they cause and what can be done about them.
www.seagrant.wisc.edu/home/Default.aspx?tabid=571

Traveling Trunks
Full of hands-on activities to teach children about nonindigenous species and how they're affecting our area.
www.seagrant.umn.edu/educators/tt

Preschool through 12th Grade Invasive Species Education
http://dnr.wi.gov/topic/invasives/edresources.html

Aquatic Invasive Species: An Educator's Information and Materials Guide
www.seagrant.umn.edu/pdfs/AIS_Resources_List.pdf

National Invasive Species Information Center
Links to educational tools for teaching K-12 students about invasive aquatic species.
www.invasivespeciesinfo.gov/aquatics/education.shtml